C000092818

KNOWLEDGE MATTERS Volume 2

A reference guide to the theory requirements
of LAMDA Graded Examinations
in Speaking Verse and Prose
from 1 September 2014

Contents

LAMDA
KNOWLEDGE MATTERS

Volume 2

KNOWLEDGE MATTERS Volume 2

Previously published as *The Discussion*: 1996, 2000, 2004 and *Knowledge Matters*: 2009
This edition first published in 2014 by the
London Academy of Music and Dramatic Art
155 Talgarth Road, London W14 9DA
Tel: +44 (0)844 847 0520 / Fax: +44 (0)844 847 0521
www.lamda.org.uk

A catalogue record for this book is available from the British Library.

Contributors: Clarissa Aykroyd, Mia Ball, Paul Bench, Jacque Emery, Greg Hamerton,
Linda Macrow, Ann Newson, Stephen Owen, Paul Ranger, John Rhys Thomas,
The Voice Care Network UK, Catherine Weate. Illustrations by Lucy Atkinson.

Printed by: CPI Group (UK) Ltd, Croydon, CR0 4YY
Cover image: Martin Burton Photography
Concept design and layout: Cambridge Design Consultants

ISBN: 9780955768781

Introduction

We have called this book *Knowledge Matters* because knowledge of interpretative skills, technical skills and literature is the foundation for performance. This is a reference book for teachers and students of speech and drama and an essential guide for learners studying for the LAMDA *Graded Examinations in Communication: Speaking Verse and Prose* (from 1 September 2014). It provides the necessary information on the set theory for all grades.

Graded Examinations in Communication: Speaking Verse and Prose

The examinations have been designed to develop the skills necessary for effective oral communication of the written word. *Knowledge Matters Volume 2* should be read in conjunction with the syllabus for *Graded Examinations in Communication: Speaking Verse and Prose*, which is available to download from LAMDA's website or to purchase in printed form.

The examinations are divided into four distinct levels, in line with the National Qualifications Framework.

National Qualifications	LAMDA Grades
Entry Level (Entry 3)	Entry
Level 1	Grade 1 Grade 2 Grade 3
Level 2	Grade 4 Grade 5
Level 3	Grade 6 – Bronze Medal Grade 7 – Silver Medal Grade 8 – Gold Medal

The set theory is listed in the Knowledge section of each grade within the syllabus.

The Knowledge section

The set knowledge requirements have been designed to introduce learners to the technical aspects of performing verse and prose. The learner's knowledge and understanding are tested in discussion with the examiner after the learner has performed their chosen selections. The examiner will aim to put the learner at ease. Questioning is more formal in the higher grades as the set knowledge requirements increase in technical difficulty.

The Knowledge section has its own learning outcome(s) and related assessment criteria.

The examiner will initiate the discussion and the learner will be encouraged to respond. This should evolve into a two-way exchange between the examiner and the learner, during which the learner will be given every opportunity to share their knowledge.

There is a time limit for the Knowledge section. However, the learner must be prepared to discuss all aspects of the set knowledge requirements for the grade being assessed.

The examiner will base their questions on the set knowledge requirements printed in the syllabus for *Graded Examinations in Communication: Speaking Verse and Prose* (from 1 September 2014). This information should be made available to the learner by the teacher so that the learner is fully prepared and is able to discuss the theory with confidence.

Practical application

This book has been designed to help the learner to understand and use background knowledge and techniques required to give a creative, enhanced performance.

Practical application of the knowledge learnt and understood will lead to a greater enjoyment of verse and prose in performance. It is therefore important that the learner relates the set knowledge to their performance as much as possible in their responses. This is particularly relevant at Grade 4 (figures of speech), Grade 5 (phrasing and pausing), Grade 7 (emphasis and modulation), and Grades 7 and 8 (versification) where the learner will be asked to illustrate the information with examples from their chosen selections whenever possible.

Speaking Verse and Prose
Knowledge Requirements

Entry Level (E3)

The learner will answer questions on the following:

- *the general content of both verse selections*

- *the meaning of four individual words taken from the two verse selections (selected by the examiner at the time of the examination).*

The general content of the verse selections

When you have chosen your poems, try to explore the meaning of them. It is important to understand them as a whole. For example:

- Do they paint a picture?

- Do they tell a story?

- What are the poems trying to say?

The meaning of the words

To understand the whole of the poem you must know the meanings of all the words. If you are uncertain of any words, try not to guess the meaning but look them up in a dictionary. Some words have more than one meaning and you can only tell which is correct from the way the word is used within the surrounding text.

Speaking Verse and Prose
Knowledge Requirements

Level 1: Grade 1

The learner will answer questions on the following:

- *the content and mood of the two verse selections*
- *the meaning of four individual words taken from the two verse selections (selected by the examiner at the time of the examination).*

Content and mood of the verse selections

To prepare, you should look at the way the pieces are written. For example:

- Are they shaped differently on the page?
- Do they have a strong rhythm?
- Do they both use rhyme?
- What is the mood of each poem?
- Is the mood different in the two poems?
- Does the poem tell a story?
- Is the poem descriptive?
- Is the poem sad?
- Is the poem humorous?
- Is it a scary, atmospheric or cheerful poem?

You may also enjoy and comment on the sounds of the words in a poem.

For your examination, it is a good idea to select two pieces of verse that differ in either theme or mood so that you are able to show some contrast when you perform them.

The meaning of the words

See Entry Level.

Speaking Verse and Prose
Knowledge Requirements

Level 1: Grade 2

The learner will answer questions on the following:

- *the story of the book from which the prose selection has been taken*
- *the content of the verse selection*
- *the mood of the verse and prose selections.*

Content and mood of the prose selection

When you have read your book, try to answer these questions:

- What happens in the story?
- Where and when is the story set?
- Do you have a favourite part of the story?
- How does the extract you are performing fit into the story as a whole?
- What is the mood of the extract you are performing?
- Does the mood change during the extract?

When discussing your book with the examiner, remember to answer the questions as fully as possible whilst being concise.

Content and mood of the verse selection

See Grade 1.

Speaking Verse and Prose
Knowledge Requirements

Level 1: Grade 3

The learner will answer questions on the following:

- *two characters (of his/her own choice) from the book from which the prose selection has been taken*

- *the content of the verse selection*

- *the mood of the verse and prose selections*

- *the fundamental differences between verse and prose.*

Choice of characters in the prose selection

When you have read your book and chosen two characters, think about the following questions:

- Why have you chosen these characters?
- Are they main characters in the story?
- What do you think these characters look like?
- What do they say about themselves?
- What happens to them and why?

Content and mood of the verse selection

See Grade 1.

Content and mood of the prose selection

See Grade 2.

The fundamental differences between verse and prose

Be able to recognise which of your selections is verse and which is prose and be able to give details as to how you can tell.

Prose is the usual form of written and spoken language. In English, words flow continuously across the page and are broken into sentences and paragraphs. Prose writing usually follows a logical sequence and a grammatical order.

Verse is immediately recognisable on the page because the words are arranged into patterns. Verse may be broken up into stanzas but this is not essential. Verse often has little grammatical order. Insignificant but grammatically necessary words may be omitted and the accepted word order changed. In some modern verse, there is little or no punctuation and even a lack of capital letters. Verse may also make more use of figures of speech, such as similes and metaphors, than prose. Verse often rhymes at line endings.

Examples of different verse patterns:

- *Aunt Jennifer's Tigers* by Adrienne Rich
- *Roller Skaters* by Grace Nichols

Prose and **verse** both possess rhythm but verse rhythm is more distinct. Rhythm is the beat or pulse you can hear when you say the words. Sometimes the rhythm is arranged in a regular pattern of stressed and unstressed syllables, which is known as **metre**. Verse rhythm can be very strong and easy to feel or quite gentle and subtle.

Some examples of verse with a strong metrical rhythm are:

- *The Word Party* by Richard Edwards
- *From a Railway Carriage* by Robert Louis Stevenson

Verse examples can be found in *The LAMDA Anthology of Verse and Prose (Volume 18)*.

Speaking Verse and Prose
Knowledge Requirements

Level 2: Grade 4

The learner will answer questions on the following:

- *the relationship between two characters (of his/her own choice) from the book from which the prose selection has been taken*

- *the content of the verse selection*

- *common figures of speech (alliteration, assonance, onomatopoeia, antithesis, simile, personification, metaphor).*

Definitions of common figures of speech must be illustrated with examples from the chosen selections or other texts.

The relationship between two characters

When you have read your book and chosen two characters, try to think about the following questions:

- What do the characters say about each other?

- What do other people say about them?

- How do the characters relate to each other?

- How does their relationship develop or change and why?

Figures of speech

A figure of speech is a non-literal expression or one which uses a particular pattern of words for emphasis. Such features are found more commonly in verse than prose, though some are used quite regularly in everyday speech without being recognised for what they are.

a) **Alliteration**. Alliteration is the repetition of an initial consonant. This can produce a striking effect when the poem is spoken aloud. One effective example of the repetition of the hard 'p' sound is found throughout the poem *Big Fat Budgie* by Michaela Morgan:

Might park on my perch
Might peck in my pot...

Clarissa Aykroyd uses the soft 's' sound for a smoother effect
when describing a sunburst in *Andalucía*:

Southern sun in stars...

b) **Assonance**. Less commonly used than alliteration, assonance
is the repetition of a vowel sound, and again it is particularly
noticeable when the lines are spoken. Repetition of the short 'u'
and 'a' sounds in *The Sea* by Daphne Lister illustrates this:

The waves come
tumbling,
rumbling,
crashing,
dashing the harbour wall...

The opening lines of Coleridge's *Kubla Khan* provide a good
example of alliteration and assonance combined:

In Xanadu did Kubla Khan
A stately pleasure dome decree:
Where Alph, the sacred river, ran
Through caverns measureless to man
Down to a sunless sea.

c) **Onomatopoeia**. Onomatopoeia is another device that makes
particular use of sounds. It refers to those words that make a
sound similar to their meaning when spoken aloud. Among
the simplest are 'pop' and 'hiss'. There are relatively few
words which really fulfil this criterion but in poetry there is
often an onomatopoeic quality to phrases which enhance the
meaning when spoken. One example is from Brian Moses' *The
Sssnake Hotel*:

And if, by chance, you lie awake
and nearby something hisses,
I warn you now, you're about to be covered
in tiny vipery kisses,
at the Sssnake hotel, at the Sssnake hotel.

Jacqueline Emery's *Midnight Cats* also concentrates on sound:

> Hissing,
> Screeching,
> Yowling,
> Tearing,
> Balls of fur
> Rolling with a loud crash!

d) **Antithesis**. Antithesis occurs when a word, phrase or idea is set in opposition to another, resulting in a strong contrast or ambiguity which can often surprise or shock. In its simplest form it is the placing of opposites beside one another, as in Shel Silverstein's *Zebra Question*:

> Are you noisy with quiet times?
> Or are you quiet with noisy times?

It is quite a dramatic device and was often used by Shakespeare. A more striking and developed example of antithesis can be seen in one of Romeo's speeches from the first scene of *Romeo and Juliet*:

> Here's much to do with hate, but more with love.
> Why then, O brawling love, O loving hate,
> O anything of nothing first create!
> O heavy lightness, serious vanity [...]

e) **Simile**. A simile is one of the most commonly used figures of speech, likening one thing to another thing. One simple and well-known example is the opening line of Robert Burns' poem:

> My love is like a red, red rose.

Another example of a simile is found in Oscar Wilde's *Symphony in Yellow*:

> And at my feet the pale green Thames
> Lies like a rod of rippled jade.

You can always recognise a simile by the use of the words 'like' or 'as'.

f) Personification. Personification is where inanimate things are endowed with human qualities. In *Ode to the West Wind*, Shelley addresses the west wind as if it is a person. Another example of personification is when Christina Rossetti refers to the moon as a person in *Is the Moon Tired?*:

> Is the moon tired? She looks so pale
> Within her misty veil...

g) Metaphor. A metaphor is more powerful than a simile because it turns one thing into something else. A clear example comes in Shakespeare's *Othello*, when Iago speaks:

> O, beware, my lord, of jealousy;
> It is the green-eyed monster, which doth mock
> The meat it feeds on.

Some metaphors are extended through an entire piece of writing. In Andrew Young's poem *Hard Frost*, the frost is seen as an army and the image is sustained through the whole poem.

Now find examples of these definitions in your chosen selections or other texts. Be prepared to talk through these examples with the examiner.

Content and mood of the verse selection

See Grade 1.

Speaking Verse and Prose
Knowledge Requirements

Level 2: Grade 5

The learner will answer questions on the following:

- *the main plot of the book from which the prose selection has been taken*
- *the content of the verse selection*
- *phrasing (sense-groups, breath-groups, parenthesis)*
- *pausing (sense pause, emphatic pause, rhythmical or metrical pause, suspensory pause, caesural pause, emotional pause).*

Definitions of phrasing and pausing must be illustrated with examples from the chosen selections or other texts.

The plot of the book

The plot is a narrative of events with emphasis on cause and effect: what happened, and why? It is the way that a story is arranged. For example, important information may be withheld from the reader or the story might not be told in chronological order.

In the classic novel *Jane Eyre* by Charlotte Brontë, the existence of Mrs Rochester is crucial to the story, although in terms of the plot it is not divulged until halfway through the book.

E M Forster defined the difference between a story and a plot: 'A story is a narrative of events in chronological order. A plot is a narrative of events with the emphasis on causality.'

The content of the verse selection

See Grade 1.

Phrasing

Grammatically, a **phrase** is a group of words which makes sense but not complete sense on its own. For example:

> The captain *of the ship* has gone on board.
> Jack was found *after a long search*.

In speech, a **phrase** consists of a group of words linked together by sense. Phrases are sometimes called 'sense-groups'.

a) **Sense-groups**. Each sense-group introduces a fresh idea. The sense-group may be one word or a number of words. To break a sense-group is to destroy the sense.

In *Death Rains* by Mary Ndlovu, we read:

> Cool rain soaks down
> Runs in streams,   [*sense-group*]
> Awakening rivers.   [*sense-group*]
> Laughter rings as
> Children's play shapes
> Dams and roads.   [*sense-group*]

b) **Breath-groups**. Breath-groups and sense-groups frequently coincide, but this is not a rule. The breath-group represents the number of sense-groups that can easily be said on one breath. The ability to adjust breathing to meet the demands of the breath-group depends on an understanding of phrasing and breath control. Breath pauses may be longer than sense pauses and should occur where a longer pause is indicated by the text (often by punctuation, such as a comma or a full stop).

Notice how the breath-groups in *Death Rains* are slightly different from the sense-groups:

> Cool rain soaks down
> Runs in streams,
> Awakening rivers.   [*breath-group*]
> Laughter rings as
> Children's play shapes
> Dams and roads.   [*breath-group*]

c) **Parenthesis**. Parenthesis occurs when a word, phrase or sentence is inserted as an explanation, an afterthought or an aside into a passage which is grammatically complete without it. It is usually marked by brackets, dashes or commas. Parenthesis can be made clear in performance with a pause before and after the group of words, or with a change in pitch, pace or volume.

In *Through the Looking-Glass* by Lewis Carroll, there is a clear example of parenthesis – the phrase between the two commas, shown here in italics:

> "Some people," said Humpty Dumpty, *looking away from her as usual*, "have no more sense than a baby!"

Pausing

In speech, a **pause** is when sound stops. There are many different types of pause which help the speaker or reader to bring meaning and mood to life.

a) **The sense pause**. The sense pause is used in connected speech to mark the sense by indicating the end or beginning of a sense-group. It is sometimes referred to as oral punctuation, but this can be misleading because it would seem to imply that it is used in the same places as written punctuation, which is not always the case.

b) **The emphatic pause**. A pause for emphasis may be made before a word or phrase, after a word or phrase, or, for extra strong emphasis, both before and after a word or phrase. The word or phrase is therefore isolated and achieves prominence. Carefully timed, an emphatic pause will build suspense and climax. Holding an emphatic pause for too long will break the sense and alienate an audience.

Observe how effective an emphatic pause is when used before the final phrase of the extract from *Half Moon Investigations* by Eoin Colfer, when the speaker realises his mistake:

The window creaked open and a tremulous voice drifted down to me.

"If you're looking for May Devereux, she lives next door."

I was, of course, outside the wrong house.

c) **The emotional pause**. In an emotional pause the voice is suspended by the strong working of the emotions. It must be used with great subtlety or it will sound overdramatic and insincere.

In *Lost Horizon* by James Hilton, there is an emotional pause before the final phrase of dialogue:

> And Conway answered, shaken with an emotion for which he knew no reason and which he did not seek to conceal: *"That you are still alive, Father Perrault."*

d) **The rhythmical or metrical pause**. Rhythmical pauses are used at the ends of lines of verse and between stanzas to indicate the form and pattern of the verse. These pauses should be timed with the rhythm of the verse. A metrical pause is also used when a line of verse is shorter than the surrounding lines so that a pause is needed to balance the rhythm and timing.

Observe the rhythmical pauses in *Colonel Fazackerley* by Charles Causley:

> Colonel Fazackerley Butterworth-Toast   [*short pause*]
> Bought an old castle complete with a ghost,   [*short pause*]
> But someone or other forgot to declare   [*short pause*]
> To Colonel Fazack that the spectre was there. [*short pause*]

e) **The caesural pause**. A caesura is a slight pause which occurs mid-line in verse, usually indicated by a break in sense and sometimes indicated by a punctuation mark. This can be seen in *The Railway Children* by Seamus Heaney in the middle of this stanza:

> We were small and thought we knew nothing
> Worth knowing. We thought words travelled the wires
>   [*caesural pause on full stop*]
> In the shiny pouches of raindrops...

f) **The suspensory pause**. A suspensory pause is indicated by no punctuation at the end of a line of verse, also known as an enjambed line. When it occurs in verse, the speaker needs to preserve the meaning without losing the rhythm or form of the verse. The last word of the first line is suspended by pitch and length, in other words, a pause on the word itself. Therefore the speaker must continue on to the next line without a breath pause.

In *Flight* by Joan Lees, several lines are enjambed and thus include a suspensory pause, as on the word 'splinters':

> Circle the lake, sun splinters
> on wooded shoreline and mountains.

Line structures in verse which affect pausing

a) **End-stopping**. In an end-stopped line, the sense and rhythm fall silent, or pause, at the end of the line. This is often indicated by a punctuation mark.

b) **Enjambment**. In an enjambed line, the sense of a line of verse continues on to the next line (the opposite of end-stopping).

Now find examples of these definitions in your chosen selections or other texts. Be prepared to talk through these examples with the examiner.

Level 3: Grade 6 – Bronze Medal

The learner will answer questions on the following:

- *the key themes in the book from which the prose selection has been taken*

- *the content of the verse selection*

- *the techniques involved in breathing, voice and basic speech production (resonance, projection and articulation).*

Themes in the book

Themes are related to plot. A theme is a recurring idea or subject in the novel. They may be broad (love) or specific (the effect of immigration on human relationships). Themes unite the characters, events and structure. For example, the events could all involve love, marriage, greed or adventure, as found in Jane Austen's *Pride and Prejudice*.

Exploring a theme does not necessarily mean coming to any firm conclusion about it. For example, in the novel *Lost Horizon* by James Hilton, unresolved questions are raised on the subject of the longevity of human existence.

The content of the verse selection

See Grade 1.

Breathing

'Breath is fundamental to life. It is also fundamental to producing voice. Because breathing is an involuntary activity, we seldom give it a thought unless it is difficult or painful. But if we hear that our voice is too soft, fades away or won't carry, we need to consider how we breathe.'

(From *More Care for Your Voice* by the Voice Care Network UK)

There are numerous bones and muscles involved in the breathing process.

a) **Bones**. The spine is made up of a series of vertebrae. The twelve pairs of thoracic vertebrae curve around to the front of the chest forming the ribcage. Seven pairs join with the sternum. Three pairs join with the seventh and two pairs are 'floating' (unattached). You can feel the definition of the ribs with your fingers.

b) **Muscles**. The *intercostal muscles* are situated between the ribs (inter = between, costal = ribs). The *diaphragm* is a dome-shaped muscle dividing the chest and the abdomen. It is attached to the lower edges of the rib cage, the point of the sternum and, at the back, the vertebrae. The *abdominal muscles* form part of the abdominal cavity and help to control the movement of the diaphragm.

c) **Breathing in**. When we breathe in, the intercostal muscles contract and move the ribs slightly upwards and outwards. The diaphragm, which is attached to the ribs, moves in response to this action, flattening out. This creates more space inside the chest, giving the lungs room to expand. As the lungs expand, the air pressure reduces and air immediately flows in through the nose or mouth in order to equalise the pressure. The abdominal muscles release and the lungs fill with air.

d) **Breathing out**. We then exhale. The muscles converge simultaneously to support the release of the breath. The abdominal muscles contract, the diaphragm rises and the ribcage returns to its original position through the relaxation of the intercostals. The lungs are compressed, and air flows out through the nose and mouth, powered by the abdominal muscles.

e) **Support**. Your teacher may have given you a direction to 'support your voice'. This means having just the right amount of pressure from the abdominal muscles to create just the right amount of breath force for the sound you want to use. For example, if you want to project your voice across a large space or to sustain a long phrase, then you will need a more consistent pressure from the abdominal muscles.

Breathing exercises will help you with this process. These should be preceded by relaxation exercises. When you practise a breathing exercise, place your hands on your lower abdomen and centre your attention there. This will help the abdominal muscles to release on the in-breath and contract on the out-breath. Taking breath from your 'centre' (an imaginary point inside your body below your navel) will also help you to relax and release the sound more freely and easily.

f) **Clavicular breathing**. This type of breathing is to be avoided. It involves moving the ribs upwards but not outwards when breathing in, holding air in the upper lungs and raising the shoulders. This sometimes happens when the body is tense, putting strain on the vocal folds. Make sure that your spine is lengthened and your shoulders, neck and jaw are free from tension.

Voice production

'Voice begins with an impulse from the brain. It is stimulated by an intention to speak or sing. Two elements produce voice – a flow of air and vibration.

The air flows from breath. Air is taken in through the mouth or nose, passes down the trachea (or wind-pipe) and into the lungs. It is drawn there by the contraction of the dome-like diaphragm. As the diaphragm relaxes, the abdominal muscles work to return breath up the trachea.

The larynx (or voice box) is located in the upper part of the trachea. Its primary biological function is to serve as a protective valve for the air-way. When we use our voice, we close two bands of muscular tissue in the larynx – the vocal folds (or cords) – across the air flow. The out-breath causes the edges of the folds to vibrate, generating sound, in a manner similar to that of air escaping from the neck of a balloon as it deflates. The edges of the vocal cords are quite short – 15–20mm – and their vibration is extremely rapid. Depending on age, sex, health and the note pitched, the vocal folds may open and close between 60 and 1000 times per second.'

(From *More Care for Your Voice* by the Voice Care Network UK)

Figure 1: The larynx (from the side)

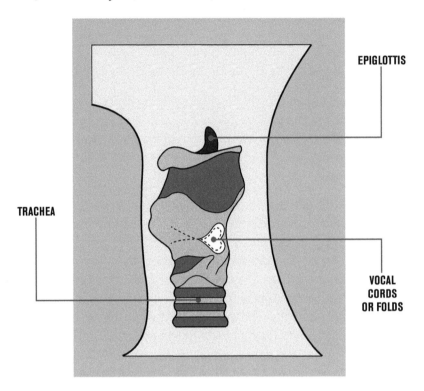

EPIGLOTTIS

TRACHEA

VOCAL
CORDS
OR FOLDS

Figure 2: The larynx (from above)

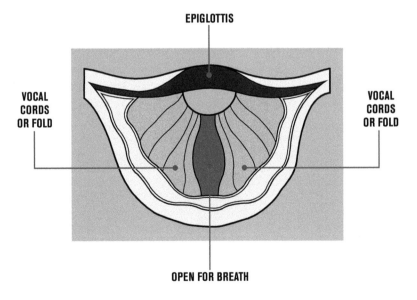

EPIGLOTTIS

VOCAL
CORDS
OR FOLD

VOCAL
CORDS
OR FOLD

OPEN FOR BREATH

Basic speech production: Resonance

The note created in the vocal folds is carried by the breath through various hollow spaces: the **pharynx** (or pharyngeal resonator), the **mouth** (or oral resonator) and the **nose** (or nasal resonator). The note is strengthened, amplified and given texture as it travels through these spaces.

a) **The pharynx (pharyngeal resonator).** This is the long muscular tube which extends upwards from the larynx, ending at the back part of the oral and nasal cavities. It is the first resonating space through which the note must pass on its way to the mouth and nose.

   The pharynx can change its shape and size, which affects the quality of the sound produced. It increases in size during a yawn and decreases in size when the throat or neck is tense.

 try this Hold a yawn in your throat and count 'one, two, three' at the same time. You will hear a sound with too much pharyngeal resonance.

b) **The mouth (oral resonator).** Each of the many parts of the mouth has a role to play in producing resonance.

   The lower jaw forms the floor of the oral resonator and is attached to the facial bones by hinge joints.

   The tongue lies on the floor of the oral resonator, rooted in the front wall of the pharynx. It is capable of intricate and rapid movements. The movement is centred in different areas: the tip (point of the tongue), the blade (underneath the upper tooth ridge), the front (underneath the hard palate), the centre (partly underneath the hard palate and partly underneath the soft palate) and the back (underneath the soft palate).

   The lips form the exit of the oral resonator at the free edges of the mouth and grip, direct and shape the breath stream.

   The hard palate is an arched bone structure, separating the oral cavity from the nasal cavities, forming the roof of the mouth.

The soft palate forms the back third of the roof of the mouth, continuing from the curve of the hard palate. The back edge is free and can move up and down. Its movement controls the flow of air through the nose or mouth, like a trap door.

When breathing naturally through the nose, the soft palate is relaxed and droops down into the mouth, which leaves the passage to the nose free. When there is an impulse to speak, the soft palate contracts upwards, blocking the passage to the nose, so that the air and sound flow through the mouth.

Say the long vowel sound 'h' with your lower jaw dropped at its most natural point. Continue saying the sound and raise your lower jaw slowly. As the lower jaw comes up, the lips will move closer together and the tongue might move towards the hard palate. You will hear a sound without much oral resonance.

Breath carries the sound from the pharynx into the mouth. If the breath force is strong enough, the sound will bounce off the hard palate and out through the lips. This is called *forward resonance*.

If the breath force is too weak to reach the hard palate, it may pitch on to the soft palate, which will make the sound difficult to project.

The mouth is capable of assuming a wide range of sizes and shapes because of the movement of the tongue, lips, jaw and soft palate. However, there needs to be space inside the mouth to create an appropriate amount of oral resonance.

Allow your lower jaw to drop at its most natural point and use a mirror to look through to the back of the mouth. If you breathe through your nose and out through your mouth with your mouth still open, then you will see the action of the soft palate.

c) **The nose (nasal resonator).** There are two types of nasal resonance:

   - when the vibrating column of air passes directly through the open soft palate to the nasal cavity: in English, this only happens on three sounds – 'm', 'n' and 'ng'

- when the vibrating column of air does not pass directly into the nasal cavity, but instead pitches on to the hard palate just behind the upper teeth, and the sound vibrations are carried through the bones of the hard palate to the nasal cavities. This type of nasal resonance can be heard in vowel sounds.

To produce the first type of nasal resonance, the soft palate must be in good working order; to produce the second type, there must be forward resonance (i.e. the breath force must be strong enough to bounce the sound off the hard palate).

If the speaker has a cold and the nasal cavities are blocked, there won't be any nasal resonance. If the soft palate doesn't close properly, too much nasal resonance will leak into the sound.

Say 'mum', 'nose' and 'sing'. Repeat the words but this time while holding your nose. You should hear 'bub', 'dose' and 'sig' because there is no nasal resonance.

d) **Balancing resonance**. Good resonance depends upon achieving a balance of vibration from the pharynx, mouth and nose. The quality of the sound will be affected if there is too much resonance from just one of the resonators.

When you practise your exercises, make sure that your spine is lengthened, your shoulders, neck and jaw are free from tension, and there is space inside your mouth and an adequate breath force to bring the sound forward. It is important that you try not to think about all of this when you are speaking or performing. You must practise your exercises so that it comes to you naturally.

The quality of sound will also be affected if the resonators are unhealthy (e.g. if you have a cold or sore throat). Unfortunately, there is little you can do to counteract the effects of illness on the quality of the sound.

Figure 3: The nose, mouth and pharynx

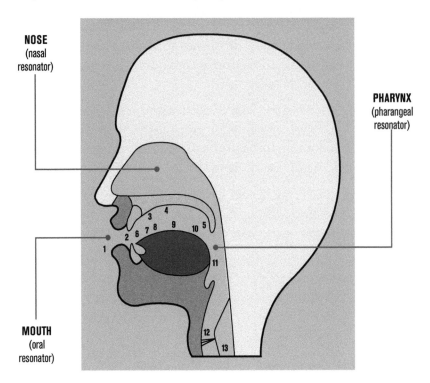

1 Lips   2 Teeth   3 Alveolar ridge   4 Hard palate   5 Soft palate
6 Tip of the tongue   7 Blade of the tongue   8 Front of the tongue
9 Centre of the tongue   10 Back of the tongue   11 Root of the tongue
12 Vocal cords or folds   13 Food passage

e) **Head and chest resonance**. You may also feel vibrations from higher notes in your head and vibrations from lower notes in your chest when you speak, which are sometimes called head resonance and chest resonance. However, the head and chest are not official resonators because the vibrations come from sound waves produced by pharyngeal, oral and nasal resonance. For this reason, head and chest resonance are sometimes referred to as *secondary resonance*.

Basic speech production: Projection

Projection involves:

a) **Audibility**

- Strong, secure breath (breath supported by the abdominal, diaphragmatic and intercostal muscles and released freely and easily)

- Forward placement of resonance (air and sound brought forward in the mouth, using the hard palate as a sounding board).

b) **Intelligibility**

- Clarity of speech (tongue and lip muscularity; precise articulation)

- Appropriate emphasis and modulation (varying use of stress, volume, pace, pitch, inflection, tone colour and pausing, according to the thought and emotion being expressed).

c) **Mental projection**

- Engaging the audience by commanding their attention, which ensures that the emotion of the words is conveyed clearly.

Basic speech production: Articulation

A good speaker is a clear speaker, whose words do not run into each other and who does not swallow word endings by speaking too quickly. Instead, the speaker ensures that words and word endings are given the full weight of sound they deserve. Good diction means clear speech.

Articulation is the formation of clear and distinct sounds in speech.

Sound is turned into speech by the use of the organs of articulation. These are the tongue, the teeth, the teeth ridge, the lips and the hard and soft palates. A vowel sound is an unobstructed sound formed by the changing shape of the mouth. A consonant sound is an obstructed sound formed by two or more of the organs of articulation coming into contact with each other. Examples of this are the consonants 'b' and 'p', when the lips come into contact with each other, or 'f' and 'v', when the teeth touch the bottom lip.

Level 3: Grade 7 – Silver Medal

The learner will answer questions on the following:

- *the key themes and any underlying themes in the book from which the prose selection has been taken*

- *the content of the poem and sonnet presented*

- *the verse form, metre and rhythm of the poem and sonnet presented*

- *emphasis and modulation (which includes stress, volume, pace, rate, pitch, inflection, tone colour and intensity).*

Definitions of emphasis and modulation must be illustrated with examples from the chosen selections or other texts.

Themes in the book

See Grade 6.

Underlying themes can also be referred to as *subtext*.

Subtext is the *internal* world. It is the hidden meaning involving knowledge, emotion and motivation. For example, in the book *Animal Farm* by George Orwell the story is about animals acting and reacting to each other, on the surface. The underlying message (the subtext) refers to the behaviour of human beings.

The content of the poem and sonnet selections

See Grade 1.

Specific verse forms

Select the appropriate verse form, metre and rhythm within it to match the poem and sonnet selected.

a) **Blank verse**. Blank verse consists of a succession of unrhymed lines which have a regular rhythm. It creates a sense of simplicity and directness, perfect for character speech and dramatic performance. Shakespeare even mentions the term in *Hamlet*:

> The lady shall say her mind freely, or the
> Blank verse shall halt for it.

Sometimes, an occasional change to the rhythm is added, in order to create variety. Hermione's trial speech in *The Winter's Tale* is in blank verse but includes a metrical change in the fifth line, which strengthens her sense of innocence:

> Since what I am to say, must be but that
> Which contradicts my accusation, and
> The testimony on my part, no other
> But what comes from myself, it shall scarce boot me
> To say 'not guilty';

b) **Free verse**. It is a common misconception that free verse is without form. Free verse possesses a structure but it is much more open and not bound by classical rules such as those found in sonnet form.

Free verse is not necessarily confined to a specific metrical law but uses a rhythm most suitable for the expression of a particular thought and emotion. For example, if the thought or emotion is profound, then the rhythm will move slowly; if the thought or emotion is trivial, then the rhythm will gallop along. A rhythmical unit of free verse is not a line but a stanza, or even the whole poem itself.

Rhyme can be included in free verse but is usually a necessary part of the thought and/or emotion. Free verse came into its own in the early 20th Century with the modernist movement. T S Eliot's *The Love Song of J Alfred Prufrock* is a particular example:

> Let us go then, you and I,
> When the evening is spread out against the sky
> Like a patient etherised upon a table;

Or Walt Whitman's *Out of the Cradle Endlessly Rocking*, taken from *Leaves of Grass*:

> Till of a sudden,
> May-be kill'd, unknown to her mate,
> One forenoon the she-bird crouch'd not on the nest,
> Nor return'd that afternoon, nor the next,
> Nor ever appear'd again.
>
> And thenceforward, all summer, in the sound of the sea,
> And at night, under the full of the moon, in calmer weather,
> Over the hoarse surging of the sea,
> Or flitting from brier to brier by day,
> I saw, I heard at intervals, the remaining one, the he-bird
> The solitary guest from Alabama.

c) Sonnet form

- **The Petrarchan or Italian sonnet**. The sonnet form is of Italian origin dating back to the Renaissance and was used by both Petrarch and Dante. The Petrarchan sonnet consists of 14 lines divided into an octave and a sestet. The octave is made up of two quatrains (sets of four lines). The sestet is composed of two tercets (sets of three lines).

  When the sonnet is written in Italian, the rhyming scheme is limited. In the octave only two rhymes are the norm: *abba abba*. Three pairs of rhymes are found in the tercet: *cde cde*.

  The *subject* consists of one idea which is stated boldly (often in universal terms) in the first quatrain and developed in the second. A pause then follows. In each of the two tercets the subject is again considered but particular details are shown. Finally, it is brought to a definite and forceful close.

The Petrarchan sonnet was introduced from Italy into England by Sir Thomas Wyatt and developed by Henry Howard, Earl of Surrey. Difficulties were encountered. Italian is a far more musical and flexible language than English and, in order to accommodate the language change, extra rhymes had to be incorporated. A second change in the form was the rearrangement of the sestet in a variety of ways: sometimes the change was in the rhyming scheme, which was altered to *cd cd cd* with the sense continued in the series of three couplets (sets of two lines) instead of spread over two tercets. In England the form became more flexible than in Italy.

An example of the English development of the Petrarchan sonnet is William Wordsworth's *Upon Westminster Bridge*:

> Earth has not anything to show more fair:
> Dull would he be of soul who could pass by
> A sight so touching in its majesty:
> This city now doth, like a garment, wear
> The beauty of the morning; silent, bare,
> Ships, towers, domes, theatres, and temples lie
> Open unto the fields, and to the sky:
> All bright and glittering in the smokeless air.
> Never did sun more beautifully steep
> In his first splendour, valley, rock, or hill:
> Ne'er saw I, never felt, a calm so deep!
> The river glideth at his own sweet will:
> Dear God! The very houses seem asleep;
> And all that mighty heart is lying still!

- **The Shakespearean sonnet**. William Shakespeare departed from the tightly interlaced model of the Petrarchan sonnet and in its place he used a form which, although it still consists of an octave and a sestet with a pause between the two, breaks into different shapes:
  - the octave is divided into two quatrains, made distinct by the rhyme scheme which runs: *abab cdcd*
  - the sestet consists of a quatrain, *efef*, and a final couplet, *gg*.

This pattern allowed Shakespeare:

- to present an argument in the octave
- to recognise either a development or a contradiction of this in the first four lines of the sestet
- to make a strong concluding statement in the couplet.

This is particularly evident in *Sonnet 97*:

> How like a winter hath my absence been
> From thee, the pleasure of the fleeting year!
> What freezings have I felt, what dark days seen,
> What old December's bareness everywhere!
> And yet this time removed was summer's time,
> The teeming autumn big with rich increase
> Bearing the wanton burden of the prime,
> Like widowed wombs after their lords' decease:
> Yet this abundant issue seemed to me
> But hope of orphans, and unfathered fruit;
> For summer and his pleasures wait on thee,
> And thou away, the very birds are mute;
> Or if they sing, 'tis with so dull a cheer
> That leaves look pale, dreading the winter's near.

Versification

Versification is the art of making verses or the theory of the phonetic structure of verse. In the English language the basic system of versification is known as **accentual-syllabic**. This describes the pattern made between the number of syllables in the line of verse and the accents placed on them. In most English poetry the verse structure is created in this way, by balancing the fixed or varying numbers of syllables in a line with the constant alternation of accented and unaccented syllables in definite, recurring sequences.

Metre and rhythm

English speech rhythm is formed by a combination of weak and strong stresses. English verse rhythm depends upon the arrangement of these stresses into patterns. When that pattern is regular and repeated, it is called **metre**.

One bar or unit of a metrical form is called a foot, derived from dancing in Ancient Greece when the foot was raised and set down on the stressed beat of a musical bar.

A metric line is named according to the number of feet:

monometer	=	one foot to a line
dimeter	=	two feet to a line
trimeter	=	three feet to a line
tetrameter	=	four feet to a line
pentameter	=	five feet to a line
hexameter	=	six feet to a line
heptameter	=	seven feet to a line
octometer	=	eight feet to a line

A metric line is also named according to the type of **rhythm** within the unit or bar. In English verse there are two main types: **rising rhythm** and **falling rhythm**.

a) Rising rhythm

- **Iambus (an iambic foot)**. An iambic foot consists of an unstressed followed by a stressed syllable:

  weak <u>strong</u> | weak <u>strong</u> | weak <u>strong</u> | weak <u>strong</u> |weak <u>strong</u> | (iambic pentameter)

  de <u>dum</u> | de <u>dum</u> | de <u>dum</u> | de <u>dum</u> | de <u>dum</u> | (iambic pentameter)

  It comes from the Greek word meaning 'to hurl' or 'to throw', used when writers of satire hurled their verse, like a weapon, at their enemies. The rhythm resembles the beating of a human heart and is very close to natural speech patterns.

Although we may not be aware of it, everyday conversation frequently falls into an iambic rhythm. For example:

I hope you take the book with you to school.
I <u>hope</u> | you <u>take</u> | the <u>book</u> | with <u>you</u> | to <u>school</u>

The ticket isn't valid for today.
The <u>tick</u> | et <u>is</u> | n't <u>val</u> | id <u>for</u> | to<u>day</u>

This is one reason why Elizabethan dramatists, who were heavily influenced by the metrical forms adopted by the Greek and Latin poets of antiquity, were attracted to it. The forward drive of the iambus also makes it ideal for ongoing narrative.

For example, Romeo speaks in iambic pentameter as he waits below Juliet's window in *Romeo and Juliet*:

But soft! What light through yonder window breaks?
But <u>soft</u>! | What <u>light</u> | through <u>yon</u> | der <u>win</u> | dow <u>breaks</u>?

Notice how the metrical structure of the line gives emphasis to the words 'soft', 'light' and 'breaks'.

- **Anapaest (an anapaestic foot).** An anapaestic foot consists of two unstressed syllables followed by a stressed syllable:

  de de <u>dum</u> | de de <u>dum</u> | de de <u>dum</u> | de de <u>dum</u> | de de <u>dum</u>

  This creates a rapid effect, driving the line of the verse forward, which mirrors the movement. An example can be seen in Lord Byron's *The Destruction of Sennacherib*:

  The Assyrian came down like the wolf on the fold;
  And his cohorts were gleaming in purple and gold:

  The <u>Assyr</u> | ian came <u>down</u> | like the <u>wolf</u> | on the <u>fold</u>;
  And his <u>co</u> | horts were <u>gleam</u> | ing in <u>pur</u> | ple and <u>gold</u>:

b) **Falling rhythm**

- **Trochee (a trochaic foot).** A trochaic foot consists of a stressed syllable followed by an unstressed syllable:

  <u>dum</u> de | dum de | dum de | dum de | dum de

  <u>Never</u> | <u>Never</u> | <u>Never</u> | <u>Never</u> | <u>Never</u>

King Lear's response upon discovering his daughter Cordelia dead is captured in the mournful, falling tone of the metre. Shakespeare often used a trochee at the start of an iambic line, which emphasises the meaning of the first word, as in *Sonnet 27*:

Weary with toil, I haste me to my bed,
<u>Wea</u>ry | with <u>toil</u>, | I <u>haste</u> | me <u>to</u> | my <u>bed</u>,

- **Dactyl (a dactylic foot)**. A dactylic foot consists of a stressed syllable followed by two unstressed syllables:

  <u>dum</u> de de | <u>dum</u> de de | <u>dum</u> de de | <u>dum</u> de de | <u>dum</u> de de

  In the following line from *Hamlet* the metre places stress on the word 'that', highlighting the reflective nature of the speech and drawing our attention to the 'question'. The use of two lighter syllables in the fourth foot rapidly moves the line forward to 'question':

  To be, or not to be, that is the question
  To <u>be</u>, | or <u>not</u> | to be, | <u>that</u> is the | <u>ques</u>tion

c) **Other rhythms**

- **Spondee (a spondaic foot)**. A spondaic foot consists of two successive syllables with equal weight:

  | <u>dum</u> <u>dum</u> |

  It is usually used in the middle or at the end of a line for extra emphasis. An example can be found in *The Rime of the Ancient Mariner* by Samuel Taylor Coleridge:

  Alone, alone, <u>all</u>, <u>all</u> alone,
  Alone on a wide, wide sea!

d) **Examples** of these feet in English prosody are as follows:

- iambus – a<u>way</u>
- anapaest – in com<u>plete</u>
- trochee – <u>du</u>ty
- dactyl – <u>mer</u>rily
- spondee – <u>old</u> <u>time</u>

e) **Blending of rhythms.** A succession of lines consisting of the same kind of metrical rhythm can be monotonous. Many poets therefore combine different rhythms to create interest. Sometimes a poem can pass from rising to falling rhythm and back again. A change in rhythm can bring a change in the meaning or mood; equally, a change in the meaning or mood can bring a change in the rhythm.

f) **Scansion.** To scan a piece of verse is to go through it line by line, analysing the number of feet and marking the weak and strong stresses. While it is not necessary to scan poems or speeches in detail, it is absolutely imperative that you have a firm grasp of the ways in which poetic structure links with thought and emotion. An understanding of metrical patterning can often provide the key to the meaning of a passage that might at first seem difficult to comprehend. If you know where the stresses fall in a given speech, you will find it easier to understand and communicate the sense of the writing.

It is important that the rules of poetic form are not applied to the exclusion of thought and emotion. Working with the rhythm and metre must be connected to feeling and impulse. Overemphasis of the metre can be to the detriment of the mood and the poet's intention.

Emphasis

Emphasis is when a speaker attaches extra prominence to a particular word or thought. It can be achieved through:

- modulation (varying use of stress, volume, pace, pitch, inflection, tone colour and pausing)
- lengthening individual sounds
- intensity.

For example, dramatic emphasis can be achieved by increasing the intensity of the breath force, building volume and widening the pitch range.

If there is *underemphasis*, speech becomes dull, flat and monotonous. Sometimes, in certain types of humour, it can be used effectively, but this should be thought of as a technique rather than the normal means of communication.

If there is *overemphasis*, speech becomes irritating and tiring to listen to.

Modulation

Modulation refers to the variations in voice and speech used by the speaker to convey meaning, mood and emotion. This includes varying the use of stress, volume, pace, pitch, inflection, tone colour and pausing.

a) Stress

Stress is when prominence is given to a particular word or syllable, usually through a combination of extra breath force, a change in pitch and a lengthening of sound.

- **Word stress**. Every word of more than one syllable has its own stress: for example, <u>dra</u>gon. Some words change meaning according to word stress: for example, <u>sub</u>ject (meaning a course of study) / sub<u>ject</u> (meaning to cause somebody to undergo something unpleasant). Compound words usually bear double stress: for example, <u>home-made</u>

- **Sentence stress**. When words are linked together, word stress changes under the influence of sentence stress. Sentence stress depends on two things:
  - The relative importance of words in the sentence, and therefore the stress, depends on the context. The more important the word, the stronger its stress. For example:

    Did she give you the book? No, <u>he</u> gave me the book.
    Did you steal the book? No, he <u>gave</u> me the book.
    Is the book hers? No, he gave <u>me</u> the book.
    Did he give you the pen? No, he gave me the <u>book</u>.

    –   The rhythm and meaning of the sentence can be changed by varying the stress. For example:

In the <u>dark</u>, <u>dark</u> <u>wood</u> sat a <u>cruel</u> <u>hairy</u> <u>giant</u>.

In the <u>dark</u>, dark <u>wood</u> sat a <u>cruel</u> hairy <u>giant</u>.

b) **Volume**. Volume refers to the level of loudness or softness with which words are spoken. There should be constant fluctuations of volume to create a well-modulated delivery, but for most work (especially verse speaking) there should be only the gentlest crescendo (becoming louder) and diminuendo (becoming softer). If too much breath force is used, then shouting will occur. Shouting lacks subtlety and can create vocal problems.

c) **Pace**. Pace variation is integral to the communication of meaning and mood. There should be constant fluctuations of pace to create a well-modulated delivery.

A slower pace can be achieved by lengthening vowels and prolonging the space between words. Words suggesting size, effort, astonishment and long periods of time can be taken more slowly. Meaningful and emotional passages tend to be taken at a slower pace. A phrase which contains several ideas might also be taken more slowly and deliberately than one with a simple idea.

A faster pace can be achieved by shortening vowel sounds and continuant consonants, and shortening the space between words. Quick, easy, little, ordinary things can be taken more rapidly. An increase in pace can also be used to build to a climax. Pace is affected by the distribution of stresses in a phrase. Lighter stressing and a more rhythmical distribution of stresses can be taken at a swifter pace.

d) **Tempo or rate**. Tempo is the overall rate, or time signature, of the writing. Pace will fluctuate considerably within the limits of the tempo used by the speaker and set by the writer.

e) **Pitch**. Pitch is the specific level of highness or lowness in a speech note. A higher pitch is often used for lighter and happier thoughts. A lower pitch is often used for sombre and sad thoughts.

f) Inflection. Inflection refers to the rise and fall in pitch of the voice during speech. As the voice rises and falls, it tends to form patterns or tunes. The two most commonly heard tunes are called **falling tune** and **rising tune**.

Falling tune. This is a simple falling pattern where the stressed syllables descend from a higher pitch to a lower one. It tends to be used for:

- complete statements
- commands
- agreement
- aggression
- strong emotion
- questions not requiring a 'yes' or 'no' answer
- end of breath-groups.

Try these examples using a falling tune:
- We are fortunate to have John Smith spending the day with us.
- Put that on the table.
- I agree with your opinion.

Rising tune. This is also a pattern of descending stressed syllables, but there is a rise of pitch on the last syllable. It tends to be used for:

- doubt
- anxiety
- surprise
- pleading
- threats
- incomplete statements
- questions requiring a 'yes' or 'no' answer
- the end of a single sense-group within a larger breath-group.

try
this

Try these examples using a rising tune:
- I'm not too sure about that one.
- Please don't leave me now.
- Would you like to come to the football match?

Inflection reflects our personality, our thoughts and our feelings. Flexible use of inflection will therefore reveal subtle changes in our moods. Use of inflection must be unconscious or speech becomes stilted. The speaker should focus on communicating meaning and mood to avoid artificiality.

g) **Tone colour**. Tone colour refers to the variation of 'light' and 'shade' in the voice. It is the result of various tensions and relaxations in the resonators and other associated muscles but is prompted by the imagination and emotion. The quality of tone therefore alters according to the feelings, which helps the listener to recognise the mood of the speaker regardless of the words spoken.

In performance, the tone colour should reflect the mood of the prose or verse, but this must be sincerely imagined or it will sound false.

h) **Intensity**. Fluctuations in intensity indicate tension and relaxation according to the prevailing mood. A performer should avoid giving a whole performance at a high pitch of intensity because it is too tiring for both the performer and the audience and the value of contrast and sincerity would be lost.

Now find examples of these definitions in your chosen selections or other texts. Be prepared to talk through these examples with the examiner.

Speaking Verse and Prose
Knowledge Requirements

Level 3: Grade 8 – Gold Medal

The learner will answer questions on the following:

- *the content of the book from which the prose selection has been taken, noting key characters and events within it*

- *the content of the poem and sonnet presented*

- *the verse form, metre and rhythm of the poem and sonnet presented*

- *the life, work and influence of William Shakespeare*

- *the life, work and context of writing of one of the other authors selected (chosen by the learner).*

The content of the book

This requires an in-depth comprehension of the chosen selection, together with the ability to concisely discuss it in detail – looking at the text and subtext of the book as a whole, with its key themes, underlying themes, details of characters and important events within it.

The content of the poem and sonnet selections

See Grade 1 and Grade 7.

Verse form, metre and rhythm

See Grade 7.

Grade 8: Prose Analysis Grid	
Author	
Key facts about author	
Period and style of writing	
Other books by author	
Book title	
General outline of plot	
Key moments within the book	
Key characters	
Main themes	
Underlying themes	
Interesting quotations from the book	
Personal evaluation of the book	

Key Biographical Details

This section includes an overview of the key aspects of the writers' backgrounds together with an appreciation of the context of their writing. Students should also be aware of the writers' other works.

The following pages provide information on the writers listed in the syllabus.

Al-Saddiq Al-Raddi

Charles Dickens

Stephen Dobyns

John Galsworthy

Graham Greene

Joanne Harris

James Hilton

Thomas Hood

Khaled Hosseini

Ted Hughes

Katharine Kilalea

Louis MacNeice

Michael Ondaatje

William Shakespeare

Joe Simpson

Derek Walcott

William Wordsworth

Al-Saddiq Al-Raddi (1969–)

Poetry – may you be a green body.
May you be a language
in which I wander
with my wings and my self.

Poetry is one of the pre-eminent art forms in the Arabic-speaking world, and Al-Saddiq Al-Raddi is one of its most outstanding practitioners. Sudan is both an African country and a part of the Arabic-speaking world. As a Sudanese writer in Arabic, Al-Raddi has a particularly keen awareness of the points of tension and harmony between different cultures, political perspectives and languages. In recent years, his poems have gained a wider readership in the English-speaking world through increased translation. Their combination of rich romanticism, social and historical awareness, and emotional honesty has appealed to many readers.

Al-Saddiq Al-Raddi was born in Omdurman, Sudan in 1969. Omdurman brought together inhabitants from many different regions and was a particularly active and creative artistic centre. When Al-Raddi was 15, the literary journal *Al-Sahwa* published one of his poems, and his teachers also took note of his considerable talent. At the age of 17 he won a major poetry competition and was elected shortly afterwards to the Sudanese Writers' Union, becoming its youngest member.

In the years following Sudan's independence in the 1950s, the country had struggled under civil war, unstable governments, severe economic problems, and increasing religious and cultural repression. Many intellectuals and artistic figures had already left during the 1970s and 1980s. In 1989, Omar Al-Bashir came to power in Sudan by means of a coup which overthrew the government of Saddiq Al-Mahdi. While Al-Mahdi's government had been unstable and the country was already wracked by civil war in the south, Al-Bashir established a military government, suspended other political parties and enforced a regime which included major political and artistic restrictions.

Although politically active, Al-Raddi has rejected the label of 'political poet'. "By nature I am political. But at heart I am an artist," he said. In the immediate aftermath of Al-Bashir's accession to power, the 20-year-old Al-Raddi and his poet friends found a way to circumvent restrictions on publication and freedom of speech. "Myself and other poets would deliver the work orally – on the spot – all over Sudan. This was a way of moving outside the state's control," Al-Raddi said. "Sometimes 3,000 or 4,000 people would come. Occasionally it was hard – especially when there were political crises – but if I was stopped then others in other places would be able to continue." Al-Raddi faced imprisonment and torture for these activities, but their impact was enormous.

In 1993 Al-Raddi became a journalist covering the arts and culture, and he subsequently became the cultural editor of the daily newspaper *Al-Ayyam*. During the 1990s, he also published his first few poetry collections, including *Ghina' al-'Uzlah (Songs of Solitude)* and *Matahat al-Sultan (The Sultan's Labyrinth)*, both in 1996. These were followed by *Aqasi Shashat al-Isgha' (The Limits of the Screen of Listening)* in 2000. This poetry was at the forefront of a relatively new style in Arabic-language literature, called 'prose poetry', although it corresponds more closely to 'free verse' in English-language writing. A powerful influence on Al-Raddi's poetry was the Sudanese writer Muhammad Abdul-Hayy (1944–89) who rejected traditional, somewhat didactic forms of Arabic and Sudanese poetry in favour of strong imagery and metaphor and a more concise means of expression. Al-Raddi's poems are often very brief, but the images and words are so well chosen that they evoke a flood of sensations and glimpses of memory. *Writing the World* opens with a bleak and remarkably evocative image:

> He has trapped himself in a blank page

while *Only* succinctly fuses sensuality, intellect and spirituality:

> Like a rumoured prophet's advent
> you slide from the ripe fruit of sleep
> afire with ideas, your flashing wit

Al-Raddi has described his method of composition as "entirely internal". He starts from a single central image and generates patterns around it, without sitting down with a pen and paper or word processor. "Sometimes working on a single poem could take a few months, just churning, working on it almost line by line – always, non-stop," he said. "After that, once the poem is completed in my mind, I write it down."

Al-Raddi came to the attention of a wider international audience when he took part in the UK-based Poetry Translation Centre's World Poets' Tour in 2005. He returned several times in the next few years and wrote new poems including *Small Fox*, *Garden Statues* and *In the Company of Michelangelo*. A translation of his longer work *Poem of the Nile* appeared in *The London Review of Books* in 2006, which was the first time that they had published work by an African poet. He also began working on a project where Arabic-language writers from northern Sudan and English-language writers from southern Sudan came together to translate each other's work. However, the political implications of this work made it difficult to move the project forward.

Also in 2006, Al-Raddi became the cultural editor of the then-liberal newspaper *Al-Sudani*. In 2007 he set up a website to highlight Sudanese and other writers, *Sudanese Ink*. His international profile grew when he appeared at the 2010 Poetry International Festival in Rotterdam. A subsequent appearance at the Petrie Museum of Egyptian Archaeology in London led to his appointment as poet-in-residence in 2012. The Petrie Museum has an important collection of artefacts from the ancient Sudanese kingdom of Meroe and Al-Raddi worked on poems in response to these items, developing his fascination with the impact of the ancient on the modern.

In the summer of 2012, Al-Raddi represented Sudan at Poetry Parnassus in London. This festival was the largest gathering of international poets ever staged, as part of the Cultural Olympiad surrounding the 2012 London Olympic and Paralympic Games. While he was in the UK, a series of mass arrests took place around an uprising in Sudan. Al-Raddi lost his job with *Al-Sudani* and would certainly have been arrested if he had been in Sudan at the time. He applied for asylum in the UK and is now living in London.

Sarah Maguire, the head of the Poetry Translation Centre and one of Al-Raddi's translators, said of his poetry: "The delight of his work is in the use of multi-layered metaphors that often refer to ancient Sudanese kingdoms in juxtaposition with contemporary observations… an ability to make connections between the ancient past and the politically charged present." His friend and fellow Sudanese poet Afeif Ismail commented: "His poetry shows a great love of the beauty of African nature, and shows great skill in enlivening classical Arabic vocabulary with modern idioms." Al-Saddiq Al-Raddi's place in the pantheon of great African and Arabic-language poets, along with his increasing popularity in other countries, have combined to make him a particularly significant poet for the challenges of the 21st Century.

Charles Dickens (1812–70)

*'Annual income twenty pounds, annual expenditure nineteen
nineteen and six, result happiness. Annual income twenty
pounds, annual expenditure twenty pounds ought and six,
result misery.'*

Charles John Huffam Dickens was born in Portsmouth, England
on 7 February 1812, the second of John and Elizabeth Dickens's
six surviving children. John Dickens worked in the Navy Pay Office
and was transferred to Chatham near Rochester in Kent when his
son Charles was five years of age. Dickens recalled years later that
these were the happiest of days, playing on farmland around his
house or travelling in a yacht with his father up the river Medway
towards the Thames estuary – a landmark that he was to use for
Great Expectations – 'dark, flat, wilderness… intersected with dykes
and mounds and gates, with scattered cattle feeding on it.' These
formative years helped to inculcate a keen sense of observation
and imagination, further developed by his mother's teaching and his
reading of books at home.

However, these idyllic times were to change when Charles was 12. His
father was transferred to London where the family was often in debt
– later inspiring Dickens to describe his father as "a jovial opportunist
with no money sense" and to use him as a model for Mr Micawber
in his novel *David Copperfield*. The young Dickens was taken out of
school and given a job in a black polish warehouse. He was never
to forget that his parents did not object to this, especially as they
paid fees for his older sister, Frances, to attend the Royal College
of Music. In addition to all of this, his father was arrested for debt
and imprisoned at Marshalsea Debtors' prison in London for three
months, although the debts were eventually paid from inheritance
money. Soon after, his father retired with a pension. Dickens was then
able to attend Wellington House Academy, a school for boys, until he
was 15.

At the age of 19 he fell in love with the daughter of a bank official but
her parents thwarted the relationship. After leaving school he became
a clerk with a law firm for a short time, learning the skill of shorthand

and becoming a parliamentary reporter. He grew to dislike the law and the lawyers in his novels are unscrupulous, including Dodson & Fogg in *The Pickwick Papers* and Uriah Heep in *David Copperfield*. He also came to believe that politicians were ineffective and that, as a writer, he could do more to help the poor.

When he was 23 years old, Dickens met 19-year-old Catherine Thomson Hogarth, the daughter of the editor of the *Evening Chronicle*. They were married in 1836 at St Luke's Church in Chelsea. Using his skills as a reporter, Dickens began to write for monthly periodicals and his pieces appeared as *Sketches by Boz*. A serialisation followed of *The Posthumous Papers of the Pickwick Club*. He was soon in demand by publishers and began to struggle to meet monthly deadlines, often feeling tired and occasionally ill. He was frustrated when he realised that his publishers were growing rich at his expense and was thankful for the support of a good friend, John Forster, who acted as an adviser and intermediary. Forster eventually became his biographer.

Dickens became the editor of *Bentley's Miscellany*, a monthly periodical to which he contributed the serialisation of *Oliver Twist*. Such was his work ethos that, before finishing *Oliver Twist* (1837–39), he started writing *Nicholas Nickleby* (1838–39), where his mother was portrayed as Mrs Nickleby. His next work was *The Old Curiosity Shop* (1840–41), in which the death of Nell Trent caused distress among the reading public. *Barnaby Rudge* (1841), a historical novel, did not prove popular. From 1846 until 1867 he also edited and contributed to the magazines *Household Words* and *All the Year Round*.

By 1842 Charles Dickens had written five novels in as many years and his stories were popular on both sides of the Atlantic. He travelled to America and later published his thoughts on American society in *American Notes: For General Circulation*, in which he was critical of the widespread spitting of tobacco, slavery and the fact that he had no international legal claim on the copyright of his work. His satirical attack on American society was portrayed in his next novel, *The Life and Adventures of Martin Chuzzlewit* (1843–44).

From 1844 to 1847 he took his family to live in Italy, Switzerland and finally Paris. On his return he acquired new publishers who rewarded him with sufficient financial prospects for the rest of his life. With Angela Burdett Coutts, a wealthy philanthropist, he established housing schemes, schools for the poor and accommodation for homeless women.

Between 1843 and 1848 he wrote five Christmas books, the first of which, *A Christmas Carol* (1843), has been considered an indictment of 19th-Century industrial capitalism. Later novels – *Dombey and Son* (1846–48), *David Copperfield* (1849–50), *Bleak House* (1852–53), *Hard Times* (1854), *Little Dorrit* (1855–57), *A Tale of Two Cities* (1859), *Great Expectations* (1860–61) and *Our Mutual Friend* (1864–65) – showcased Dickens' increasing artistic maturity.

In 1856 Gad's Hill Place, a house that had appealed to Dickens as a child, came up for sale and he bought it for £1,700. It was to remain his home until his death.

Charles and Catherine Dickens had ten children but they separated in 1858 when he developed a relationship with a young actress, Ellen Ternan. In 1865 Dickens was involved in a serious train crash and in 1867–68 he revisited America to give more readings. His health was now deteriorating and he suffered minor strokes. He was working on his fifteenth novel, *The Mystery of Edwin Drood*, when he died at Gad's Hill on 9 June 1870, and he was buried in Poets' Corner at Westminster Abbey. Catherine outlived Dickens and died from cancer in 1879. She gave a collection of their letters to her daughter Kate with the injunction: "Give them to the British Museum, that the world may know he loved me once."

Adverse criticism of Dickens' work tended to focus on sensationalism and sentimentality. However, the success of his early books owed much to the popular appeal of their comedy and pathos and their attacks on notorious public abuses. The depth, range, complexity and style of his later novels forged the development of the novel as a literary form, causing Tolstoy to describe him as the greatest novelist of the 19th Century.

Admired by contemporaries as varied as Queen Victoria and Dostoevsky, Dickens was such an entertaining writer that it was a century before he was taken seriously. Academics have since remedied this.

Stephen Dobyns (1941–)

"I can't believe there is a poet who hasn't eagerly put down a word one day, only to erase it the next day deciding it was sheer lunacy. It's part of the process of selection. As for the fellow in the poem, what he does may be comic, but he himself is very serious. He's a sliver of the human condition."

Stephen Dobyns's narrative, long-line poetry is known for its wry and conversational voice and for its use of sometimes surreal perspectives to shed light on human hopes, fears and foibles. Also a successful reporter and author of fiction and non-fiction, this American poet is adept in the use of storytelling as a vehicle for metaphor and for the musicality of the language.

Stephen Dobyns was born in 1941 in Orange, New Jersey. His father was an Episcopalian minister who had also been a musician, and his mother and brother were both interested in music. His family moved several times during his childhood and adolescence, so that he lived in various states including Michigan, Virginia and Pennsylvania. "My mother would recite poems to me from last century," he said. "There were a lot of books in the house. In school, I didn't particularly like poetry. We mostly read 19th-Century poetry and there was a sense it was in a code… I was one of those kids who sat in the back row and didn't pay attention and didn't respond to Emerson's poetry."

From the age of about 15, Dobyns developed a real interest in poetry when he discovered that there were performers who fused jazz and poetry, including the likes of William Carlos Williams, Walt Whitman and Langston Hughes. Around this time, Dobyns started to read poetry by T S Eliot, Wallace Stevens and Emily Dickinson, among others. He also read science fiction, the works of Ernest Hemingway and other fiction. Although some of his teachers encouraged his writing, he was uncertain as to whether he wanted to pursue writing as a career until he started college.

Dobyns studied at Shimer College, Illinois, and Wayne State University, Michigan, before receiving his MFA (Master of Fine Arts) from the Iowa Writers' Workshop at the University of Iowa. He started writing novels, the third of these being a mystery novel which he was able to publish. While still continuing to write poems, he became a reporter for the *Detroit News*, which would lead on to work writing feature stories for the *San Diego Reader*. "I probably learned more about writing from journalism than I did studying for an MFA," he said. "In journalism the edits were so fierce... It all goes back to sentences – how do you say something exactly. In poetry, fiction and journalism, you're trying to translate the world into language and are always looking for more exact ways to do it."

His first book of poetry, the relatively surreal *Concurring Beasts*, was published in 1972. Out of his more than ten poetry publications, subsequent collections have included *The Balthus Poems* (1982), narrative poems based on the paintings of the Polish-French artist Balthus, and *Pallbearers Envying the One Who Rides* (1999). This latter volume is a series of poems based on a character named Heart, who represents a sort of everyman. In the poem *Can Poetry Matter?*, Heart reflects on the potential of poetic forms:

> *Lyric poetry means teamwork, thinks Heart: a hog farm,*
> *corn field, and two old dobbins pulling a buckboard of song.*

In a more recent volume, *The Porcupine's Kisses* (2002), Dobyns explores the possibilities of maxims in providing inspiration for poetry. "I like aphorisms, maxims, phrases. I've read them from several dozen different writers from the Argentine writer Borges to Marcus Aurelius to all kinds of people, and so I was thinking in those terms, and I started writing some, and I saw I could work a few of them into prose poems. Some of them became definitions, and I saw that I could do a whole section of definitions, and basically I was learning a new way to approach a certain subject matter."

Dobyns has taught at institutions in the United States including Sarah Lawrence College, Warren Wilson College, the University of Iowa, Syracuse University and Boston University. He has also been the recipient of fellowships from the Guggenheim Foundation and the National Endowment for the Arts. As a fiction writer, he has written many acclaimed short stories and novels, many of which are detective stories. Dobyns is also the author of a collection of essays on poetry called *Best Words, Best Order* (first published in 1996). In this book, Dobyns explores poets such as Osip Mandelstam and Rainer Maria Rilke, and looks at both the technical and the more mystical aspects of poems and poetry writing.

With a voice which holds appeal both for readers who look for accessible poetry and for more exacting critics, Stephen Dobyns continues to write with a curious and playful outlook on the poetic craft. "I suppose there's a need to translate my experience of the world into language. Things are most palpable to me in language," he says. "Obviously, we live within time, and time is constantly going by, and a poem or anything you write, really, attempts to freeze a moment of time. I've always felt a need to do that as well... something I saw, something I experienced. The poem is not necessarily directly about that experience, but it is a metaphor for it, and, too, there's the pleasure of putting the words together, of trying to articulate things in a particular manner, whether it be in the complexity of image or the complexity of sound. That's always a task: to see if you can do that."

John Galsworthy (1867–1933)

'The finality that is requisite to Art, is not the finality of dogma, nor the finality of fact, it is ever the finality of feeling, of a spiritual light subtly gleaned by the spectator out of that queer luminous haze which one man's nature must ever be to others.'

John Galsworthy was an English novelist and playwright whose literary career spanned the Victorian, Edwardian and Georgian eras. He was appointed a member of the Order of Merit in 1929, after earlier turning down a knighthood, and was awarded the Nobel Prize for Literature in 1932 'for his distinguished art of narrative which takes its highest form in *The Forsyte Saga*.' Still popular today, his works can be read both as entertaining fiction and as a reflection of and commentary on many important issues of his era.

Born into a wealthy and well-established family with a large estate in Kingston upon Thames, Galsworthy attended Harrow School and New College, Oxford. He read Law, trained as a barrister and was called to the bar in 1890. He was not keen to practise or to make a career of the law, however, and instead travelled abroad as part of the family's shipping business. During his travels he met Joseph Conrad, the great Polish writer, with whom he formed a lifelong friendship. At the age of 28 he began writing for his own amusement and his first stories were published under the pseudonym John Sinjohn, although they were later withdrawn. In 1895 he began a romantic affair with Ada Pearson, who was the wife of his cousin Major Arthur Galsworthy. She divorced Arthur and she and John were married in September 1905, staying together until his death in 1933. At the outbreak of World War I, Galsworthy was 47 years old. Too old to fight, he worked in France at the Benevole Hospital for disabled soldiers and also signed over his family house as a rest home for members of the British Army recovering from war injuries.

Galsworthy was a skilled dramatist. He often wrote about specific social issues such as the problems of capitalism and social inequality, reflected in works such as *The Silver Box* (1906) and *Strife* (1909). *Justice* (1910), his most famous play, contributed to prison reforms in England. His feelings about World War I were expressed in *The Mob*

(1914), in which the voice of reason is submerged by the people's desire for war. Each play is built on a frame of ideas and this notion of the problem drama appealed to him very much. His legal education and training must surely have stood him in good stead here and the pros and cons of a case are presented forcefully and clearly. The drawing of characters is firmer than in his novels. Reduced to essential elements, the plots proceed with more energy and the dialogues keep halfway between the mere photography of familiar conversation and the conventional language of the stage.

Galsworthy took himself even more seriously as a novelist than as a playwright and possibly his most famous work is the trilogy entitled *The Forsyte Saga* (1922), about a family who are presented to the reader as a ruthless force united not by the bonds of affection but by greed and an almost tribal hostility to those outside the family. These books, and many of his other works, deal with social class, particularly the vagaries of the middle and upper classes. Galsworthy also looks closely at human relationships, particularly troubled marriages. The character of Irene in *The Forsyte Saga* is drawn to a certain extent from Ada Pearson. Although he shows understanding and sympathy towards his characters, Galsworthy also highlights their repellent attitudes, prejudices and hypocrisy. Commentators have noted the important influence that Tolstoy had on Galsworthy. Tolstoy's diatribes against privilege, wealth and social injustice aroused a genuine response in Galsworthy's own experience and observation.

He is viewed as one of the writers of the Edwardian era who led the way in challenging some of the norms and ideals of Victorian society and literature. Galsworthy is also regarded as an important figure as far as the development of English fiction is concerned, if only because he demonstrated the extent to which middle-brow, 'bestseller' standards were increasingly affecting profounder values and insights.

A television series of *The Forsyte Saga* broadcast by the BBC achieved immense popularity in Great Britain in 1967 and later in many other countries, especially the United States. This adaptation helped to revive public interest in an author whose reputation had unfortunately declined after his death. There have been other, more recent television and radio adaptations of *The Forsyte Saga* which have also been successful and which continue to showcase the work's popularity.

In addition to writing many important literary works, Galsworthy was also a renowned social activist. He was an outspoken advocate for the women's suffrage movement, prison reforms and animal rights. He became the president of an organisation that sought to promote international cooperation through literature.

Galsworthy died from a brain tumour on 31 January 1933. The French literary academic Louis Cazamian wrote of him: 'His temperament was that of a complete artist, rounded off by the emotions of a noble heart and the disquietude of courageous thought. The exceptional quality of his work is due to the width of its range. Each note, in itself, is not free from some analogy with tones already heard; but it rings with a very pure sound, and the whole scale has the mellowness of a delightfully original art.'

Graham Greene (1904–91)

'A stranger with no shortage of calling cards, devout Catholic, lifelong adulterer, pulpy hack, canonical novelist, self-destructive, meticulously disciplined, deliriously romantic, bitterly cynical, moral relativist...'

(From an article about Graham Greene in *The Nation*)

Henry Graham Greene was a British writer, playwright and literary critic. He was born in 1904 at St John's House, a boarding school in Hertfordshire, where his father was a housemaster. He was bullied at school and became very depressed, attempting suicide on a number of occasions. At the age of 16 he was sent for psychoanalysis in London, which was a radical course of action for the time. He probably suffered from what we now know as bipolar disorder, which had a profound effect on his writing and personal life.

Greene attended Balliol College, Oxford, where he was a contemporary of Evelyn Waugh. He graduated with a second-class degree in History and converted to Roman Catholicism in 1926, which enabled him to marry Vivien Dayrell-Browning, the woman he loved at the time. Greene admitted to her later that he had great difficulty believing there was a God at all. He retained a cynical attitude to the Church for the rest of his life. Dayrell-Browning later said: "With hindsight, he was a person who should never have married." Greene always strongly objected to being described as a Roman Catholic novelist, rather than a novelist who happened to be Catholic. Religious themes are at the root of much of his writing, especially in the four major novels *Brighton Rock*, *The Power and the Glory*, *The Heart of the Matter* and *The End of the Affair*. Other works show an avid interest in the working of international politics and espionage.

In London, Greene worked as a journalist, editor and critic for *The Times* and *The Spectator* in the 1920s and 1930s. During World War II, he was employed in the propaganda section of the Ministry of Information and was later recruited into MI6, the Secret Intelligence Service. One of his friends, as well as his supervisor, was Kim Philby, a high-ranking figure in MI6 who would later be revealed as a notorious double agent for the Soviet Union. Greene found many aspects of intelligence work frustrating, whether stationed in London or in Sierra Leone, West Africa. Following his resignation from MI6 in 1944, he continued to work as a freelance journalist, travelling to and working in countries such as France, Poland and Vietnam. The settings of his books were as far-flung as his travels.

It has been said that, of all the novelists of the 1930s, Greene was the most responsive not only to the spirit but to the atmosphere of the times. He highlighted the never-ending moral struggle between good and evil. Many of his plots directly reflected events of the day: the financial manipulation of Ivan Krogh in *England Made Me* (1935) was suggested by the career of Kreuger, the Swedish 'Match King'; *Brighton Rock* (1938) sprang from the Brighton Race Gang murders; *The Confidential Agent* (1939) was set against the background of the Spanish Civil War; and *The Power and the Glory* (1940) derived from the anti-clerical governorship of Tabasco in Mexico.

As Arthur Calder-Marshall, himself a distinguished writer of the same era and beyond, has pointed out: "The source material for Graham Greene's novels might have been the '*Police Gazette*', '*The News of the World*' and the files of '*Mass Observation*'." One of the criticisms levelled against Greene is that he is too preoccupied with the squalid and the seedy, but it must be realised that the era of the slump, of gangster rule in Italy and Germany, of the concentration camps, of Civil War in Spain, of the hypocrisies and evasions of non-interventionism was squalid and seedy. Greene was simply writing and recording it as it was.

Greene was not merely an ephemeral journalist, however, and his uncompromising realism is not just a matter of surface and temporary detail. His style has the effect of conjuring up a scene in a palpable and almost compulsive way that at times reminds one of Dostoyevsky.

A volume of his letters published after his death revealed that Greene's personal life was one of decadence and even hypocrisy. He was an alcoholic and a serial womaniser who dabbled in opium smoking and stronger drugs. Noel Coward said of him: "He has a strange, tortured mind." Despite his chequered life, Greene's accomplishments were such that he was awarded the Order of Merit and created a Companion of Honour by the Queen.

During his final years, Greene lived in Vevey, Switzerland, where he was friends with the actor Charlie Chaplin. In March 1991, suffering from a form of leukaemia, Greene was rushed into hospital in Switzerland, where he died at the age of 86.

Graham Greene was undoubtedly one of the greatest novelists of the 20th Century and his influence on the cinema and theatre was enormous. He wrote five plays and many of his exciting and exhilarating novels have been successfully brought to the screen. He is regarded by academics and critics alike as one of the master storytellers of his age, presenting topical work with atmosphere and realism. Some of his characters, such as the murderous Pinkie in *Brighton Rock* and the elusive Harry Lime in *The Third Man*, stay so vividly in the public consciousness that they are assured of immortality. Perhaps the same might be said of Greene himself.

Joanne Harris (1964–)

"The relationship between writer and characters is often quite a troubled one. At times it's a kind of benign possession, with certain individuals conspiring to take over control of the plot from their hapless creator and take it wherever they want to go."

Joanne Harris, one of Britain's most popular contemporary authors, writes about themes and subjects that intrigue her, and which she hopes will inspire her readers to question her characters and their motives. Her main objective as a writer is to create a reaction in her reader and stir up feelings. Throughout her career as a writer, she has achieved these goals with engaging stories, memorable settings and quirky characters.

Joanne Harris was born in Barnsley, Yorkshire, in 1964 and first lived in her grandparents' sweetshop. Her French mother and English father were both academics, teaching Modern Languages at a local grammar school. Although she has never lived in France, Harris's first language was French and she spent all her childhood holidays there while her grandfather was alive. It is therefore not surprising that France is the setting for many of her novels.

After school she studied Modern and Medieval Languages at St Catherine's College, Cambridge. Following teacher training, she taught Modern Languages at Leeds Grammar School and lectured on aspects of French literature and film at Sheffield University. Harris worked in education for 15 years. When her mother learned of Harris's desire to become a writer, she pointed out that the majority of writers whose books were on their shelves died penniless. Nevertheless, during this time Harris had three books published including *Chocolat*, a dark magical modern folk tale set in France. The success of *Chocolat* led her away from teaching and into a career of full-time writing.

Both her mother's and father's families had traditions of strong women, folklore and storytelling, gardening and cooking. These all contributed to the variety of themes and genres in Harris's writing, which include literary fiction, magic, fantasy, faith and superstition.

Her first novel, *The Evil Seed*, was published in 1989. Set in and around Cambridge, this novel is a reworking of the classic vampire myth. The story was a direct response to her mother's distrust of anything approaching horror or sci-fi. Although it achieved only minor success, *The Evil Seed* paved the way for her second book, *Sleep, Pale Sister*, published in 1994. In this book Harris demonstrates a much stronger sense of structure, and a style of writing which had developed from horror to a more literary, supernatural gothic tale.

It was the great success of *Chocolat*, published in 1999, that really established Joanne Harris's place in modern literature. When creating a synopsis for the book, Harris knew she wanted to write about family (inspired by her maternal grandmother, a strong influence on Harris and a wonderful cook). "I wanted to write a book about that conflict between indulgence and guilt, with chocolate as the central metaphor," says Harris. She also wanted to concentrate on themes of people and community. *Chocolat* emerged as a dark modern folk tale which captured the reader's imagination.

Chocolat earned the number one spot on the *Sunday Times* bestseller list. The book won the Creative Freedom Award in 1999 and was shortlisted for the 1999 Whitbread Novel of the Year Award. The movie rights were sold to Miramax Pictures and the success of the motion picture starring Juliette Binoche and Johnny Depp brought Harris worldwide recognition. Two other novels in the Chocolat series follow the adventures of Vianne Rocher: *The Lollipop Shoes* (2007) and *Peaches for Monsieur le Curé* (2012). In addition, together with *Chocolat*, the novels *Five Quarters of an Orange* (2001) and *Blackberry Wine* (2004) are known as the Food Trilogy. The principal setting of *Blackberry Wine* is the same village as in *Chocolat*.

Runemarks (2007) is a fantasy novel based on Norse mythology, aimed at both adults and children. The sequel, *Runelight*, was published in 2011. In the same year, Harris published *Holy Fools*. The idea for this book came from a French history text which made reference to the reform of an Abbey in Port-Royal by a newly appointed Mother Superior of only 11 years of age. Her other novels include *Gentlemen & Players* (2005) and *Blueeyedboy* (2010).

Many of Harris's earliest memories are about food. Her childhood holidays were spent on the French island of Noirmoutier and she recalls visiting markets in the early mornings and cooking sardines on a charcoal brazier on the sand. Her recollections are frequently associated with the tastes and smells of cooking. These early experiences contributed to her collaboration on two cookery books with Fran Warde: *The French Kitchen* (2002) and *The French Market* (2005).

In 2005 she published a collection of short stories, *Jigs and Reels*. The colourful characters in these tales include, to quote the book's blurb, 'suburban witches, defiant old ladies, ageing monsters, suicidal Lottery winners, wolf men, dolphin women and middle-aged manufacturers of erotic leatherwear'. Harris continued to explore this genre alongside her novels, and her second collection of short stories, *A Cat, A Hat and a Piece of String*, was published in 2012.

Her books are now published in more than 40 countries and she has won many British and international awards. In 2004 she was one of the judges of the Whitbread Book Awards and in 2005 she was a judge of the Orange Prize.

Joanne Harris lives with her husband and daughter about 15 miles from where she was born and still plays bass guitar in a band first formed when she was 16. She has said that her hobbies include "mooching, lounging, strutting, priest baiting and quiet subversion of the system". Harris also claims that she buys "far too much perfume, is slightly obsessed with musical theatre, gets on well with bishops and archbishops but is still waiting for an audience with the Pope!"

James Hilton (1900–54)

'Never had Shangri-La offered more concentrated loveliness to his eyes; the valley lay imagined over the edge of the cliff, and the image was of a deep unrippled pool that matched the peace of his own thoughts.'

Although James Hilton is not as famous today as he was in the first half of the 20th Century, his novels and screenplays of adventure and love exerted a major influence on popular culture which continues to be felt today. His writing resonates with the impact of the two World Wars and with the longing for romantic and utopian ideals in a world that was changing with increasing speed and savagery.

Born in Lancashire, England, Hilton grew up in the London suburb of Walthamstow, where his parents were schoolteachers. As a teenager, he attended the Leys School in Cambridge, where he wrote for and edited the school magazine. These years of his life coincided with World War I and some of the stories that he wrote had to do with war themes, especially as many of the older students found themselves in battle. Later, he wrote of this time period: 'It was a frantic world; and we knew it even if we did not talk about it. Slowly, inch by inch, the tide of war lapped to the gates of our seclusion.'

Hilton studied literature and history at Christ's College, Cambridge University, graduating with an honours degree in English. He was still an undergraduate student when his first novel, *Catherine Herself*, was published in 1920. After finishing his studies, he pursued journalism and worked for newspapers including the *Manchester Guardian*, the *Daily Telegraph* and the *Irish Independent*. During the 1920s, he lived with his parents and wrote several novels, but these did not achieve much success. "I was not exactly overburdened with royalties," he later commented wryly. His first really successful novel was *And Now Goodbye* (1931), a love story, followed by *Knight Without Armour* (1933), a romantic espionage story set around the Russian Revolution.

Lost Horizon was also published in 1933 and made Hilton famous. In 1934 it won the prestigious Hawthornden Prize for the best work of imaginative literature. This great success was followed by the novella *Goodbye, Mr Chips* in 1934, which was commissioned by the *British Weekly* and proved enormously popular in both Britain and America. Hilton wrote *Goodbye, Mr Chips* in only a few days and based the character of Chips on popular schoolmasters whom he had known at the Leys School, particularly the senior classics master W H Balgarnie. "Balgarnie was, I suppose, the chief model for my story," Hilton said. "When I read so many other stories about public school life, I am struck by the fact that I suffered no such purgatory as their authors apparently did, and much of this miracle was due to Balgarnie." Following on the success of *Lost Horizon* and *Goodbye, Mr Chips*, Hilton's earlier novels were reissued to meet his new audience's demand.

Shortly after his marriage in 1935 to his girlfriend Alice Brown, a BBC secretary, Hilton was invited to move to California to work on screenplays in Hollywood. He was received as a celebrity in the United States. In Hollywood, Hilton became part of the extensive British expatriate community and made California his home, never returning to live in England. He worked on screenplays such as *Camille* (1936) and *Foreign Correspondent* (1940), and won the Oscar for Best Screenplay for *Mrs Miniver* (1942).

Hilton was friends with Hollywood stars such as Frank Capra, Ronald Colman and Greer Garson. Ronald Colman starred in the film adaptation of *Lost Horizon* (1937), directed by Frank Capra; Hilton did not write the screenplay for this film, but he was one of the advisers. In 1942, Colman also starred with Greer Garson in a film adaptation of the novel *Random Harvest*, first published in 1941. One of Hilton's most popular works, *Random Harvest* tells a deeply moving and romantic story of a man traumatised by shellshock in World War I, in the context of the months leading up to World War II. As with many of Hilton's other works, *Random Harvest* is imbued with nostalgia for a world uncomplicated by violence and war, and a longing for a more idyllic lifestyle. However, the subject matter and intent of his novels ranged widely; *We Are Not Alone* (1937) is about anti-foreign sentiment during World War I and became a film (with a screenplay by Hilton) in 1939.

Hilton's first marriage fell apart in 1937, and he married the young actress Galina Kopineck only a week after his divorce. This marriage also ended eight years later, and Hilton ultimately reunited with Alice Brown. Sadly, he died prematurely of liver cancer in 1954, having been cared for by Alice during his illness.

Today, James Hilton's novels are generally considered to be popular entertainment rather than great literature, but they are still notable for their fluid, descriptive style, memorable scenes and carefully drawn characters, which raise them above many similar works of the 1930s and 1940s. References to 'Mr Chips' and 'Shangri-La' are still abundant in popular culture. The fact that these places and characters have their origins in Hilton's writing is not always remembered, but in some respects that is an even greater testament to their enduring cultural effect; it seems as though Mr Chips and Shangri-La must have been entirely real. Films such as *Lost Horizon* and *Random Harvest* are considered classics and have also helped to keep Hilton in the popular consciousness.

Thomas Hood (1799–1845)

'Next to being a citizen of the world, it must be the best thing to be born a citizen of the world's greatest city.'

Thomas Hood may be regarded as one of the most considerable and original influences among the minor poets of the Victorian era. He was also an editor, a publisher and a humorist. Born in London in 1799, the son of a bookseller, he was educated privately until the age of 14. When his father died in 1811, Hood was sent to work in a counting house. He was always a delicate and ailing boy, causing a later literary critic to say: 'His life was one long story of suffering, fraught with troubles, and he appears to have been a creature singled out by fate for affliction.' His poor health forced him to move to Dundee in Scotland to recover with relatives. Seven years later in 1818 he returned to London to work as an engraver. The nature of the work was difficult for this less than hardy youth and at the age of 21 he became the subeditor of the famous *London Magazine* after the editor John Scott was killed in a duel.

His earlier literary works included *Lycus and the Centaur*, a striking piece of imaginative writing, the *Plea of the Midsummer Fairies*, a graceful and charming work, and the grimly powerful and melodramatic *Eugene Aram*. From the beginning of his writing his sensitive disposition was balanced with a sparkling humour. As proof of his literary vocation, he used to write out his poems in printed characters, believing that this approach helped him to understand his own faults and quirks of character. At heart, though, he was a serious writer, with a vivid sense of the more seamy side of life. He had the literary skill to present this with simple and homely power. His poem *The Song of the Shirt*, perhaps his most famous piece, and *The Bridge of Sighs* exhibit a gift for dealing with human problems in a popular manner, without the sentimentality usually associated with popular verse of this type and time:

With fingers weary and worn,
With eyelids heavy and red,
A woman sat in unwomanly rags,
Plying her needle and thread –
Stitch! Stitch! Stitch!
In poverty, hunger and dirt,
And still with a voice of dolorous pitch,
She sang 'The Song of the Shirt'.

Work! Work! Work!
While the cock is crowing aloof!
And work – work – work,
Till the stars shine through the roof!
It's Oh! to be a slave
Along with the barbarous Turk,
Where woman has never a soul to save,
If this is Christian work!

(From *The Song of the Shirt*)

The pulsating rhythms of this lament for a poor London seamstress, published anonymously in *Punch* in 1843, struck a telling blow against one of the worst social abuses of the day. In this poem, the romantic feeling of individual suffering is extended into social compassion.

In 1824 Hood married Jane Reynolds and collaborated on *Odes and Addresses* with his brother-in-law J H Reynolds. Hood and his wife had two children: a girl, Frances, and a boy, Tom, who became quite a well-known playwright and editor in his own right.

Hood was also associated with and a regular contributor to the *Athenaeum*, which was a widely read literary and scientific periodical, published between 1828 and 1923. It grew into one of the most influential periodicals of the Victorian era, eventually becoming the *New Statesman*. It is regarded by historians as a mirror of its time, containing reviews, articles, essays and reports of learned societies and news from the scientific and political worlds.

Hood wrote humorously on many contemporary issues, as he and his family were always in need of money, and it was this side of his work which brought the greatest financial rewards. A good example of this is when he addressed the serious problem of grave-robbing and the selling of corpses to anatomists in an unusual and witty way:

> *Don't go and weep upon my grave,*
> *And think that there I be.*
> *They haven't left an atom there*
> *Of my anatomie*

He also succeeded in lighter poems, such as the famous and much-loved anthology piece *I remember, I remember*:

> *I remember, I remember*
> *The house where I was born,*
> *The little window where the sun*
> *Came peeping in at Morn*

Another poem, *The Haunted House*, is a good example of Hood's excellent imaginative powers:

> *No human figure stirred, to go or come,*
> *No face looked forth from shut or open casement;*
> *No chimney smoked – there was no sign of Home*
> *From parapet to basement.*

Prolonged illness brought further financial difficulties for Hood. Sir Robert Peel, the prime minister, gave Hood's wife £100, a very large sum of money at that time, to help with the family's debts (without her husband's knowledge). This is surely a testament to Hood's popularity.

Financial considerations often compelled Hood to work in a lighter vein, although he was a genuine humorist and a great lover of puns. Happily, his fortunes improved before he died, enabling him to work for a while in his serious style. Some of his strongest work belongs to his later years. Starting as a poet in the classical vein popular at the time, his verse soon caught the humanitarian fire that marks the poetry of the earlier Victorian era. Indeed, he may be thought of as a poet of the new democracy.

Khaled Hosseini (1965–)

'... but better to be hurt by the truth than comforted with a lie.'

Khaled Hosseini was born in Kabul, Afghanistan. His father was a diplomat and his mother a history teacher. They moved from Afghanistan to France in 1976 because of his father's diplomatic work. After a violent communist coup in Afghanistan and invasion by the Soviet army, the family sought political asylum in the United States.

Hosseini studied at Santa Clara University where he earned a bachelor's degree in Biology, followed by a medical degree from the University of California. He completed his residency and was a practising intern between 1996 and 2004.

While in medical practice, Hosseini began writing his first novel, The *Kite Runner*, which meant getting up very early in the morning to write for two to three hours before going to work. The book was published in 2003 and became an international bestseller. It spent more than two years on the *New York Times* Bestseller List and was adapted as a successful film in 2007.

The Kite Runner is the story of a young boy, Amir, struggling to establish a closer rapport with his father and coping with the memories of a haunting childhood event. Amir has a close friend who grew up with him in Kabul – Hassan, the son of his father's servant. Hassan is a Hazara, a member of a shunned ethnic minority. When the Soviets invade and Amir and his father flee the country for a new life in California, Amir thinks that he has escaped his past, but he cannot forget Hassan. The novel explores themes of betrayal, the price of loyalty, and the ethnic tensions between the Hazara and Pashtun in Afghanistan. Written against the backdrop of Afghanistan's history from the final days of the monarchy until the collapse of the Taliban regime, it describes the rich culture and beauty of a land in the process of being destroyed. Ultimately, though, it is a novel about redemption.

The Kite Runner was a word-of-mouth success that took some time to build a sales momentum. Hosseini continued working as an intern even as sales of *The Kite Runner* soared to over 18 million copies worldwide. He was reluctant to give up the security of a job and still found it hard to believe that his writing career would last. He had no intention of quitting medicine and becoming a writer, but the demands of both careers became too heavy. "When my patients would come in to visit me, more out of a sense of getting a book signed than getting their diabetes treated, I started to see the writing on the wall." It was time to become a full-time writer.

His second novel, *A Thousand Splendid Suns*, was published in 2007 and also hit number one. Whereas *The Kite Runner* dealt with brotherhood and fatherhood and the lives of men, *A Thousand Splendid Suns* addresses the issues confronting women. The two main female characters in *A Thousand Splendid Suns* were inspired by Hosseini's sense of what women in Afghanistan went through, particularly following the withdrawal of the Soviets and the outbreak of anarchy, extremism and criminality.

When Hosseini travelled to Afghanistan in 2003, he accumulated a diverse range of vivid eyewitness accounts and heartbreaking stories. At the time he did not realise that his encounters would provide inspiration for a book. He mainly hoped to learn about the country, as he had been out of Afghanistan for 23 years. He spoke to many boys and women in the street, learning about what they had gone through. "There's been so much written about Afghanistan, but so little about the inner life of the people living in those situations," said Hosseini in an interview.

In 2013 Hosseini published his third novel, *And the Mountains Echoed*. The first inspiration for the book was a haunting image that appeared in his mind of a desert at night, with a man pulling two children – a brother and sister – in a wagon. "My new novel is a multi-generational family story as well," he said, "this time revolving around brothers and sisters, and the ways in which they love, wound, betray, honour, and sacrifice for each other."

Hosseini's own experience of Afghanistan is quite different from the Afghanistan of his books. He has nothing but fond memories of his upbringing in Kabul, where he had a very rich social life, being part of a large extended family. It was a peaceful era before the Soviet invasion. Life revolved around being with people. Kabul was a thriving cosmopolitan city with an active intellectual life. Even in those early days Hosseini was writing stories. He was raised in a highly literate family, his parents could recite poetry and there were lots of books around the house. He began writing short stories and plays that were produced for gatherings of friends and family. Reading and writing have always been a major part of his life, and he considered himself a writer long before he chose to study medicine. Among his many writing influences he lists Persian poetry, Lewis Carroll's *Alice in Wonderland* and John's Steinbeck's *The Grapes of Wrath*.

In 2006 Hosseini was named a goodwill envoy to United Nations High Commissioner for Refugees (UNHCR), which is a United Nations agency mandated to protect and support refugees and assist in their voluntary repatriation, local integration or resettlement. He has also established the Khaled Hosseini Foundation, which works with UNHCR to help refugees and to provide assistance and opportunities particularly for the women and children of Afghanistan.

Hosseini lives in California with his wife and two children. He plans to continue writing for as long as he can, saying: "The only fear that I have is what if that goes away… I do live with the very real possibility that we don't have endless stories to tell." Most importantly, he wants to continue writing out of experiences – whether his own or those of other people – which are personally meaningful: "Everything that happens [in my books] happens because I feel it… Whatever the readers feel when they're reading my books, I feel it tenfold when I'm writing it."

Ted Hughes (1930–98)

'Every poem that works is like a metaphor of the whole mind writing, the solution of all the oppositions and imbalances going on at that time. When the mind finds the balance of all those things and projects it, that's a poem… What counts is that it be a symbol of that momentary wholeness.'

Ted Hughes is one of the towering figures of British and world poetry of the late 20th Century, although his turbulent personal life often overshadowed the brilliance of his work. Throughout his prolific career, Hughes worked not only as a poet but also as an editor, translator and author of children's books. His poetry resounds with the power of nature and the animal world, and with the strongest cadences of the English language.

Hughes was born in Mytholmroyd, Yorkshire, in 1930. His family later moved to Mexborough and his childhood brought him very close to nature and to animals. He was originally fascinated by hunting but, when he started writing poetry seriously in his teens, he found that writing was a better way to capture the essence of living animals. He spent 1949 to 1951 working as a mechanic for the RAF, which gave him ample time to read Shakespeare, the poems of W B Yeats, and others.

Hughes was a student at Pembroke College, Cambridge. Initially, he studied English, but he found the atmosphere of literary analysis to be restrictive, and he moved on to major in Anthropology and Archaeology. He also started to publish his first poems. In 1956, while launching the literary magazine *St Botolph's Review*, he met the young American poet Sylvia Plath, who had come to study at Cambridge on a Fulbright Scholarship. The attraction between them was instantaneous. "We kept writing poems to each other," Plath later said. "Then it just grew out of that, I guess, a feeling that we both were writing so much and having such a fine time doing it, we decided that this should keep on." They were married a few months after their first meeting.

Plath helped Hughes with the submission of his collection *The Hawk In the Rain* (1957) to The Poetry Center's first publication competition, where it won first prize. Faber & Faber published the book after their director T S Eliot championed it. In one of its most beloved poems, *The Thought-Fox*, Hughes describes both a living fox and the process of creative writing:

> *Brilliantly, concentratedly,*
> *Coming about its own business*
>
> *Till, with a sudden sharp hot stink of fox*
> *It enters the dark hole of the head.*

Over the next few years, Hughes and Plath lived in America and England. They both taught at institutions in Massachusetts, later returning to Yorkshire, London and then Devon. They had two children, Frieda (who inspired the famous poem *Full Moon and Little Frieda*) and Nicholas. Hughes released *Lupercal* in 1960, followed by another collection, *Wodwo*, in 1967. These collections extended Hughes's fascination with nature; the poem *Wodwo* evokes the Wild Man who roams through the history of British and European literature. Hughes also wrote reviews, essays, and work for the BBC, and he won further awards.

The marriage of Hughes and Plath became increasingly troubled and they separated in 1962, after Plath learned that Hughes was having an affair with Assia Wevill. Plath committed suicide in London in 1963, and the trauma of this event contributed to the cessation of Hughes's poetic output for several years, although he continued to be involved with the poetry world in Britain and internationally. When he started writing again, Hughes worked on the *Crow* sequence, which reflected his interest in shamanism and the esoteric. *Crow* (1970) also brought violent, primal themes to the fore, in a harsh and jagged style. The tragedy of this decade culminated in the suicide of Assia Wevill, who also killed the little daughter, Shura, she had with Hughes. In 1970 Hughes married Carol Orchard. They lived in Devon and remained married until his death.

Hughes's work continued to be imbued with a reverence for nature, alongside an awareness of its elemental darkness and brutality. He ran the small Rainbow Press during the 1970s with his sister Olwyn.

In 1984 he was appointed Poet Laureate and held the position until his death. Hughes also worked on translations of European and classical plays, such as *Tales from Ovid* (1997), and he became known for his writing for children. This included both poems and stories, but his most famous children's book is an early work, *The Iron Man* (1968), about the mysterious involvement of an iron giant in the affairs of humanity. The anthology which Hughes edited with Seamus Heaney, *The Rattle Bag* (1982), is considered one of the greatest poetry anthologies of all time.

Hughes's last major publication was astonishing to many. *Birthday Letters* (1998) was made up of poems addressing Sylvia Plath, their relationship and its breakdown. Honest and wrenching, the collection caused a sensation. It was widely praised, but many argued that its perspective was one-sided. Plath's suicide never ceased to haunt Hughes: he was often criticised for editorial decisions made regarding her work after her death and for his role in the tragedy.

Only a few months after the release of *Birthday Letters*, Hughes died of cancer in 1998. In 2011 he was commemorated in Poets' Corner in London's Westminster Abbey, with a memorial stone including lines from his poem *That Morning*:

> *So we found the end of our journey.*
>
> *So we stood, alive in the river of light*
> *Among the creatures of light, creatures of light.*

Ted Hughes' reputation has continued to grow since his death, and he has also left a considerable legacy through his championing of creative writing and poetry. His bleak and forceful style, which is also beautiful and evocative, has exerted an enormous influence upon many poets. At Hughes's funeral, Seamus Heaney said in tribute: "No death outside my immediate family has left me feeling more bereft. No death in my lifetime has hurt poets more. He was a tower of tenderness and strength, a great arch under which the least of poetry's children could enter and feel secure. His creative powers were, as Shakespeare said, still crescent. By his death, the veil of poetry is rent and the walls of learning broken."

Katharine Kilalea (1982–)

"Once, I gave up my job and tried to be a poet, but getting up every morning with nothing to do but write felt like stepping out of the world and into a kind of madness."

South African poet Katharine Kilalea, while still at an early stage of her career, has already established herself as a distinctive and unusual voice in contemporary poetry. Her poems show an intense and playful focus on the details of everyday life, seen through a rather surreal lens. These details then open up to explore the complexities of relationships, of human interactions with nature, and many other subjects.

Born in 1982, Katharine Kilalea grew up in South Africa and went to university in Cape Town. Poetry had entered her life at a relatively early age. "I remember very clearly the first poem I ever wrote," she said in an interview. "It came to me one night, lying in bed, when I was about thirteen. Suddenly a series of phrases started to circle in my head. They went: 'Standing at the crossroads / I watched the world go by. / Nobody sees the standing figure / but it feels their laughing breath.' I felt the need to get up and write them down, partly to be able to go to sleep, and partly so I didn't lose them." In 2005 she was working in a design agency in Cape Town when she decided to move to London to study for an MA in Creative Writing at the University of East Anglia. She has lived in London ever since and has also worked as a publicist for an architects' firm.

Kilalea had been writing poetry seriously at least since 2000, the year when some of the poems which would go into her first collection were written. While living in London, she sent some of her poetry to the journal *PN Review*, where they were read by editor Michael Schmidt, also the editor of poetry publishers Carcanet. He was so impressed that he asked to see more of her work and suggested that she should consider publishing a collection. The eventual result was Kilalea's first collection, *One Eye'd Leigh*, published in 2009.

One Eye'd Leigh was shortlisted for the 2009 Costa Book Awards, a considerable accomplishment for a first book of poetry. Various poems evoke the landscapes and details of London and South Africa.

In poems such as *You were a bird*, she approaches the difficulties and delights of relationships through idiosyncratic, poignant imagery:

With you there, sitting there in my kitchen,

the cooking pots start to sing.
Now the letterbox is a bird
and the telephone is made of birds when it rings.

Poetry Review said of *One Eye'd Leigh*: 'A wonderful example of original writing. She develops forms, illustrates objects, creates portraits and experiments stylishly with noticeable passion.'

Kilalea also became known for her distinctive style at poetry readings and recitals, where she generally recites poems from memory. "Mostly I have the poems memorised because I often walk around reciting them while I am writing, so they are usually quite sunk in by the time they are done," she said. "The problem with reciting from memory is that it's harder to tell if people like the work or not, because you end up talking about techniques for memorising poems."

Having already appeared on the BBC and at various poetry festivals and workshops around the UK, Kilalea was asked to represent South Africa in 2012 at London's Poetry Parnassus. This international poetry festival was part of the Cultural Olympiad surrounding the London 2012 Olympic and Paralympic Games, and it brought together as many poets as possible to represent the Olympic countries. This was a great honour which brought Kilalea's work to a wider audience, although her feelings about representing her home country were not entirely unmixed. "I usually deny being a South African poet," she said. "Particularly when one is finding one's voice and point of view, as I am, a big part of the writing process seems to be about trying to get a sense of what's around you and then doing the opposite – demarcating one's poems out from other poems. When I was at university, I took pains to find ways of writing which were unlike the South African poets we were learning about. But of course rebellion is still a way of relating."

Kilalea's more recent work has included the long poem *Hennecker's Ditch*, which appeared in Carcanet's *New Poetries V* and Salt Publishing's *The Best British Poetry 2011*, and which has been compared to T S Eliot's *The Waste Land*. Poets and poetry readers hope to see more of her work in the near future. Ukrainian-American poet and critic Ilya Kaminsky said of her work: "Kilalea writes like a painter who has also listened to a lot of music – and now can make it all her own. And she makes it like no one else. This is a new poet to watch."

Louis MacNeice (1907–63)

"Poetry in my opinion must be honest before anything else and I refuse to be 'objective' or clear-cut at the cost of honesty."

Although Louis MacNeice is often remembered as a contemporary and friend of W H Auden, Stephen Spender and Cecil Day-Lewis, readers and critics in recent decades have rediscovered his work in its own right and have ranked him alongside other great Irish and British poets of his era, particularly the pre-World War II period.

MacNeice lived in Ireland as a child, but thereafter spent most of his life in England. He felt caught between his Irish roots and the wider possibilities offered by life in England and elsewhere, and much of his poetry mirrors this tension. Like William Butler Yeats, he drew heavily on his personal experiences to create what some critics have termed 'psychodrama'. He recognised the deep influence of his childhood years, pointing to the 'early stratum of experiences which persists in one's work just as it persists in one's dreams'. Precise, witty, ironic, vehement, sometimes bitter, his poems reflect his view that a poet should be a kind of journalist of experience and emotion, leaving readers to make up their own minds.

MacNeice was born in Belfast, Northern Ireland, in 1907 and spent most of his childhood in Carrickfergus. He was an avid reader from an early age and began writing poetry when he was seven years old. His father was a Protestant clergyman and MacNeice's feelings towards faith remained ambiguous throughout his life. His mother suffered from depression and this cast a long shadow over his childhood.

After his mother's death and his father's remarriage, MacNeice was educated in England. At Oxford University's Merton College, he met Auden, Spender, Day-Lewis and others, and began publishing his poetry. He married Mary Ezra in 1930 and began working as a lecturer in Classics at Birmingham University.

MacNeice published *Poems* in 1935. Championed by T S Eliot, who accepted the collection for Faber & Faber, his work gained increasing attention. Poems such as *Valediction* and *Belfast* convey feelings about Ireland which are bitter and divided but still reluctantly loving.

Wolves hints at the gathering European storm clouds of the pre-war years, while *Snow* is a sensuous glance at the nature of perception and poetic reality:

> *World is crazier and more of it than we think,*
> *Incorrigibly plural...*

In the same year, his marriage fell apart and MacNeice was left with the couple's young son. The departure of his wife was a blow, but MacNeice continued to write poetry and to try his hand (with varying success) at playwriting, as well as travelling to Spain with Anthony Blunt and Iceland with W H Auden. The latter trip produced *Letters From Iceland* (1937), a collaboration between MacNeice and Auden.

In 1938 he published a new collection, *The Earth Compels*, and a number of prose works. By far the most important of these was *Modern Poetry*, which touched on his own approach to writing and defended the work of his contemporaries. It contains his famous remarks about the desirable attributes of a (male) poet: 'I would have a poet able-bodied, fond of talking, a reader of the newspapers, capable of pity and laughter, informed in economics, appreciative of women, involved in personal relationships, actively interested in politics, susceptible to physical impressions.' Commenting on the personal element in poetry, he wrote: 'However much is known about the poet, the poem remains a thing distinct from him. But poetry being firstly communication, a certain knowledge of the poet's personal background will help us to understand him, for his language is to some extent personal.' All of this is a fair description of MacNeice's own poetic approach.

In 1939 MacNeice published *Autumn Journal*, a long poem in 24 cantos and written in quatrains. *Autumn Journal* is still considered one of his greatest works, if not the greatest. It vividly describes his life in London, and the wider European experience, in the months leading up to World War Two. During the war years, MacNeice spent some time teaching in America, published more poetry and wrote *The Poetry of W B Yeats*, which is still acknowledged to be a significant study of Yeats. He also joined the Features Department of the BBC and remained with them until his death, working as a scriptwriter on cultural programmes, and producing plays and journalism. His collections of poetry during this time included

Plant and Phantom (1941) and *Springboard* (1944). These collections were influenced by the war atmosphere and included themes of both hope and pessimism, as well as questions of faith, as in the title poem of *Springboard*. In 1942 he married the actor Hedli Anderson.

In 1950 MacNeice went to Athens in Greece as Director of the British Institute, after which he stayed on for some time with the British Council. His experiences inspired some poetry, but his work in the 1950s is generally considered less successful than that of the 1930s and 1940s. In his final collections, *Solstices* (1961) and *The Burning Perch* (1963), MacNeice moved towards lyric poetry which reprised themes from his childhood, the realities and difficulties of his life's many relationships, and tender poems focusing on his final love, actress Mary Wimbush. W H Auden described these late poems as some of his very best. Accompanying sound engineers in Yorkshire to record sound effects for his radio play *Persons From Porlock* in August 1963, MacNeice caught bronchitis, which developed into viral pneumonia. Tragically, he did not seek medical help soon enough and he died in hospital in September 1963.

MacNeice's reputation has continued to move out from under the shadow of Auden and his contemporaries, and many feel that some of his finest work would have followed if not for his untimely death. His work has been a particularly strong influence on the great contemporary Northern Irish poets, including Derek Mahon, Paul Muldoon and Michael Longley. These poets are able to frame public and universal themes in a manner which is also personally specific, just as MacNeice did. He was also remarkably honest about himself and about the times he lived in, providing a detailed view into the atmosphere and events of the 1930s in particular, as seen in *Autumn Journal*. Irish poet and critic Thomas McCarthy commented in his essay *When I Think of MacNeice*: 'What MacNeice taught us was that sense of duty: that all who write carry an obligation to gather enough momentum to present, however briefly, a report of the true self.'

Michael Ondaatje (1943–)

'I believe in such cartography—to be marked by nature, not just to label ourselves on a map like the names of rich men and women on buildings. We are communal histories, communal books.'

Michael Ondaatje is a writer who moves between worlds. In his life and work, he has lived in and explored different countries, and the varying genres of poetry and prose, fiction and non-fiction. He juxtaposes and plays with the interactions between his characters' internal perceptions and the sensual details of the physical world around them, as well as the continual shifts in the characters' perspectives. Ondaatje is considered one of the most significant contemporary Canadian writers, but he also has profound connections to Sri Lanka and England. He has been shaped by the sensibilities of the Romantic poets, visual art, multiculturalism and many other influences, but his style continues to be highly individual and distinctive, even groundbreaking.

Michael Ondaatje was born in 1943 in Colombo, Sri Lanka. His father was the superintendent of a tea and rubber plantation, while his mother was a dancer. The marriage was not a happy one, and in 1954 Ondaatje moved to England with his mother. Educated for some years at Dulwich College in south London, he moved to Canada in 1962 and studied first at Bishop's University in Quebec. He subsequently studied for a BA at the University of Toronto and obtained his MA at Queen's University in Kingston, Ontario. He taught for a few years at the University of Western Ontario. In 1971 he took up a position in the Department of English at York University in Toronto, where he taught for many years.

Ondaatje knew from a young age that he wanted to be a writer. However, his first love was poetry. He started to publish poems in the early 1960s and released his first collection, *The Dainty Monsters*, in 1967. Ondaatje's first major publication was *The Collected Works of Billy the Kid: Left-Handed Poems* (1970), which won a prestigious Governor General's Award. Not precisely a collection of poetry, *The Collected Works of Billy the Kid* combined poems, prose, performance scenes, photographs, and elements of other artistic and journalistic genres. It was later adapted for the stage and produced as a play in Canada and the United States.

He continued to write poetry through the 1970s and 1980s and also released his first novel in 1976, *Coming Through Slaughter*. Based on the life of the jazz musician Buddy Bolden, the novel's structure reflects the style of jazz music and the protagonist's fragmenting mental state. His next novel was *In the Skin of a Lion* (1987), which looks at immigrant experience in Toronto in the early 20th Century. It was the following novel, *The English Patient* (1992), which won the Booker Prize, that made him a world-famous literary figure, particularly after it was made into a much-praised and beloved film by Anthony Minghella in 1996. Some of the characters from *In the Skin of a Lion* appear in *The English Patient*. Poetic, poignant and challenging, this novel is set at the end of World War II and explores the effects of war and the nature of various relationships, with much of the action taking place in non-chronological flashback. 'The writing is so heady that you have to keep putting the book down between passages so as not to reel from the sheer force and beauty of it', wrote reviewer Cressida Connolly in *The Spectator*.

"Poetry is a very tight machine. As William Carlos Williams says, you say it in the least number of words," says Ondaatje. "It also has to suggest bigger things than the words you used in the poem... I like the landscape of a novel, so that rather than building a big room, you are building a big house. In poetry it is one voice, or one intimate whisper, and I love that element to it, but I try to take some of that element into my fiction." During his writing career, Ondaatje has written more collections of poetry than novels; unsurprisingly, the novels have gained greater fame. He identifies both with Canada and with Sri Lanka: "I'm somebody who was born in Sri Lanka, so I'm always asked about Sri Lanka and the situation there, but I kind of avoid it. I'm somebody that lives 4,000 miles away, so I can't be a representative. I think as a writer, I'm an unofficial voice." However, some of his writing has engaged very closely with Sri Lanka, such as *Anil's Ghost* (2000), a novel with elements of mystery which looks at the country's long history of conflict from the perspective of a Sri Lankan who returns to her country after a long absence. Ondaatje's most recent novels are *Divisadero* (2007) and *The Cat's Table* (2011), and his latest poetry collections include *Handwriting* (1999) and *The Story* (2006). His novels, while apparently fictional, often have elements of autobiography.

As well as his poetry and novels, Ondaatje has edited collections of verse and prose, including *The Long Poem Anthology* (1979) and *The Faber Book of Contemporary Canadian Short Stories* (1990). His work as an editor has been particularly praised for drawing attention to the experiences of multicultural Canada, and he has also produced films and written about film editing. All of his work reflects his interest in combining genres and breaking down the walls between different artistic mediums.

"There are some writers who know exactly what the book is going to be before they write it," says Ondaatje. "Writers I really admire. But that would bore the hell out of me. It has to be an adventure. You have to discover things and learn things in the process of writing. What keeps you going is your curiosity." In a career spanning several decades, continents and genres, and recognised by many awards and honours, Ondaatje has continued to push boundaries in his writing and produce work of remarkable insight and beauty. He is one of the relatively rare contemporary writers who have reached a wide and popular audience while continuing to write with great personal integrity and innovation.

William Shakespeare (1564–1616)

'Life's but a walking shadow, a poor player, that struts and frets his hour upon the stage, and then is heard no more; it is a tale told by an idiot, full of sound and fury, signifying nothing.'

William Shakespeare lived at a time when drama had been successfully developed into a formal structure. It was also an age of exploration, and he explored the psyches of a wider range of individuals than any other writer before or since. The tension between the highly structured form and his sympathy for the inner life of his characters enabled him to push back the boundaries of drama to an unprecedented degree. His sense of dramatic structure improved as he wrote, and he stands as a model of economy and precision, both in his thoughts and in his manner of expressing them.

Controversy surrounds what little we know of Shakespeare's life. Born and educated in Stratford-upon-Avon, England, he was the son of middle-class glove-maker John Shakespeare and well-born Mary Arden. William Shakespeare married Anne Hathaway and they had three children – Suzannah, Hamnet and Judith.

He moved to London and worked in one of the theatres there. By the early 1590s he was established as part of the Lord Chamberlain's Men (later known as the King's Men). He wrote nearly 40 plays before retiring to New Place in Stratford around 1612.

Shakespeare was an actor and is believed to have played roles in his own plays, among them the Ghost in *Hamlet* and Duke Senior in *As You Like It*. He wrote many of his leading roles for the King's Men's leading actor, the flamboyant Richard Burbage. By 1598 Shakespeare was sufficiently prominent to share in the establishment of the new Globe Theatre.

Shakespeare's works include a cycle of history plays covering English history from *Richard II* to *Henry VIII*; a series of Roman tragedies (*Julius Caesar, Titus Andronicus, Antony and Cleopatra* and *Coriolanus*); a clutch of comedies including *Twelfth Night, The Merchant of Venice, The Taming of the Shrew, Much Ado About Nothing* and *As You Like It*; the celebrated tragedies *Hamlet, Macbeth, Othello* and *King Lear*;

as well as plays which are less easy to categorise – bitter comedies such as *Measure for Measure* and *Troilus and Cressida* and fables of forgiveness and redemption such as *The Winter's Tale* and *The Tempest.*

Shakespeare is remarkable in that he never presents us with his own opinions in a character's mouth. He always writes the character from the character's own point of view, and the language and vocabulary of each individual are coherent and consistent. His other remarkable innovation was his characterisation of women.

He has not always been regarded as a great dramatist. There were times when he was considered very poor, even vulgar and crude, and both Dryden and Pope wrote 'improvements' of his plays. Many of his speeches are well known and countless lines have passed into everyday language.

As well as writing plays, Shakespeare wrote a magnificent collection of sonnets, mysteriously dedicated to Mr W H (widely believed to have been a wealthy and good-looking young man), whose identity is the subject of much scholarly debate. Had he not been a playwright, the *Sonnets* and passages of *The Rape of Lucrece* would have placed Shakespeare in the front rank of Elizabethan poets.

Shakespeare's vocabulary is remarkable. Otto Jesperson, in *The Growth and Structure of the English Language*, estimates that he had 21,000 words against Milton's 8,000 and the Old Testament's 4,800. The modern 'educated' person has perhaps 2,000, of which 700 are said to comprise the normal vocabulary of the average individual.

He had become prosperous by the time he retired and died, bequeathing his wife, Anne, his second-best bed – a quirky entry in his will which has given rise to fascinated speculation ever since.

Much of Shakespeare's life is shrouded in mystery, so it is important for the reader to conduct research and draw their own conclusions. There are numerous books published on Shakespeare's life, times and works.

Joe Simpson (1960–)

'The sound of a striking clock exists only because of the silence that came before. Music is wrought half from silence, half from sound. Mountains have always been my half-silences. The peace and beauty of the valley meant nothing to me without the sombre, foreboding presence of the mountain wall above.'

Now retired from mountain climbing, Joe Simpson is well known for his colourful life as a mountaineer, a writer and a motivational speaker. His works of non-fiction and fiction deal with or are inspired by his own experiences and are famous not only for their visceral style but also for their psychological and technical insights into the challenges and rewards of extreme mountain climbing. *Touching the Void*, his first book, is viewed as one of the most important mountaineering books of all time, bringing the sport and its literature into much sharper focus for the general public.

Joe Simpson was born in 1960 in Kuala Lumpur, Malaysia, to Irish and British parents. His father was in the British Army and it was inevitable that his childhood would involve many temporary homes around the world, including Malaysia, Germany and Gibraltar. An adventurous child who was often in trouble, Simpson started rock climbing as a young teenager and found particular inspiration in *The White Spider* by Heinrich Harrer. *The White Spider*, one of the great classics of mountaineering literature, traces the history of the various climbing attempts on the North Face of the Eiger. At the time, Simpson found some of the accounts in the book so harrowing that he swore to stick to rock climbing rather than moving on to extreme mountaineering.

Simpson studied English Literature in Edinburgh and tried winter climbing in the Scottish mountains. Eventually choosing to abandon his degree studies as he saw no future in them, he climbed Alpine routes in France and Italy. He survived an avalanche in the French Alps in 1982. In 1983 he and his climbing partner hung for 12 hours over an abyss when a ledge gave way on the Bonatti Pillar. It was while he was climbing a new route on Siula Grande in Peru with Simon Yates in 1985 that he experienced the terrible events which would later be described in *Touching the Void*.

Throughout several rounds of surgery and physiotherapy, Simpson was told repeatedly by doctors that his injuries would make a return to climbing impossible. Although he chose not to believe this, Simpson was at first hesitant to start climbing again, and the deaths of mountaineering friends made it even more difficult to contemplate. A friend suggested writing a book about the experience to confront what had happened, while also recognising that the story had great commercial potential. Tony Colwell, an editor of mountain writing at the publisher Jonathan Cape, agreed to take on the book, which was published in 1988 as *Touching the Void*.

In 1989 *Touching the Void* won the Boardman Tasker Prize for Mountain Literature (a prestigious award given to the year's most outstanding contribution to mountain literature). Writing in the *Sunday Times*, George Steiner called it 'a document of psychological, even philosophical witness of the rarest compulsion'. The success of *Touching the Void* was to change Simpson's life entirely. "The great thing was that I discovered that I could write," he said. Sales of the book had been fairly slow before the Boardman Tasker Prize, but paperback editions and a very successful US publishing deal followed. *Touching the Void* also won the NCR Award, then the UK's major non-fiction award. 'There must been something in what I had said that touched people, just as I had been touched by living through the painful times I described,' Simpson later wrote.

Following on from the success of *Touching the Void*, Simpson turned to fiction and wrote *The Water People*, published in 1992. *The Water People* explores spirituality and life-and-death questions through the story of two young climbers in the Himalayas. Over the next few years, he wrote other works of non-fiction about mountaineering. *This Game of Ghosts* (1993) dealt with his early life, more dramatic climbing experiences, his activism with organisations such as Greenpeace and his career as a writer. As well as describing climbing experiences, *Storms of Silence* (1997) looked at man's inhumanity to man and particularly the plight of modern Tibet. *Dark Shadows Falling* (1997) contemplated the ethical dilemmas of mountaineering and its dark side, particularly regarding the commercialisation of Everest and its moral impact on climbers.

In 2002 Simpson published *The Beckoning Silence*, his last non-fiction book to date. An account of his attempt on the famous and deadly Eiger North Face, it was also inspired by the deaths of many of his friends over the years, through climbing and other extreme sport accidents. "I often wondered why we had chosen to play such risky games with our lives. The nearest explanation that I had for why we climbed was because it let us edge along that fine line between life and death, because for a brief moment it changed our perspectives on life," he wrote. Simpson's most recent book is another mountaineering novel, *The Sound of Gravity* (2011). Much of his work now is as a motivational speaker, bringing his inspirational stories to the corporate sector. *Touching the Void* became a very successful documentary-style film in 2003, winning the Alexander Korda Award for Best British Film at the 2003 BAFTA (British Academy of Film and Television Arts) Awards and also featuring at the 2004 Sundance Film Festival.

The intensity of Simpson's writing style, combining the immediacy of his remarkable experiences with more introspective contemplation, has made him popular even among members of the reading public who would not consider pursuing such mountaineering adventures. Often considered a niche area, mountaineering literature has gained a great deal from his success.

Derek Walcott (1930–)

Where are your monuments, your battles, martyrs?
Where is your tribal memory? Sirs,
in that grey vault. The sea. The sea
has locked them up. The sea is History.

Derek Walcott is thought by many to be one of the greatest poets of our times. Poet Sean O'Brien calls him 'one of the handful of poets currently at work in English who are capable of making a convincing attempt to write an epic'. A Nobel Prize winner who has taught on both sides of the Atlantic Ocean, Walcott is primarily known as a poet but has also written many successful plays and essays. His work reflects a deep (and sometimes critical) love for the Caribbean while also encompassing British and other European and classical influences. The presence of the sea is everywhere in his work. Both personal and universal, his poems are also multicultural and international in a way that few other modern writers or artists have achieved.

Walcott was born in St Lucia, one of the Windward Islands of the Caribbean, in 1930. Both of his parents were of mixed racial and cultural backgrounds, and the Walcott family was deeply interested in the arts, all factors which would have a profound impact on the poet he would later become. His mother, who was a teacher, recited poetry, and there was a great variety of books around the house. His father painted watercolours and also wrote poetry. The family's Methodist faith also had a powerful influence on his life.

The young Walcott explored painting, but he felt from an early age that his calling was to be a poet. His first poem was published in the local newspaper, *The Voice of St. Lucia*, when he was 14. It proved to be controversial: "I wrote a poem talking about learning about God through nature and not through the church," Walcott later said. "Of course, to see your work in print for any younger writer is a great kick. And then the paper printed a letter in which a priest replied (in verse!) stating that what I was saying was blasphemous and that the proper place to find God was in church." At 19, he self-published his first collection, *25 Poems*, which was quite successful and earned back the money he had borrowed to publish it. He became a teacher for a few years and went on to study at the University of the West Indies in Jamaica. He also studied in the United States and then moved to Trinidad, where he founded the Trinidad Theatre Workshop in 1959.

In a Green Night: Poems 1948–1960 was published in 1962 and brought Walcott international recognition. It was followed by works such as *Another Life* (1973), an autobiography in verse, and *Sea Grapes* (1976). In *Another Life*, Walcott describes an epiphany which he calls 'a frequent experience in a younger writer. I felt this sweetness of melancholy, of a sense of mortality, or rather of immortality, a sense of gratitude both for what you feel is a gift and for the beauty of the earth, the beauty of life around us.'

Walcott's plays were also widely produced in the United States and elsewhere from the 1970s onwards. He has now written more than 20 plays, and these have been well received. However, he has expressed some frustration with the reception of his plays in cultural terms: "I am not defined as a black writer in the Caribbean, but as soon as I go to America or the UK, my place becomes black theatre. It's a little ridiculous. The division of black theatre and white theatre still goes on, and I don't wish to be a part of any one of those definitions." In the 1980s Walcott began teaching at Boston University, where he founded the Boston Playwrights' Theatre and also received a MacArthur Foundation Fellowship. As well as Boston, Walcott has taught at American universities including Harvard and Yale, while still keeping his home in St Lucia.

Omeros (1990) is considered by many critics and Walcott enthusiasts to be his most important work. Loosely based on Homer's *Iliad*, it is an epic poem recounting the conflicts between fishermen and their families in St Lucia, and it also draws on themes such as colonialism and its legacies. As elsewhere in his work, the presence of the sea and the beauty of the Caribbean are important influences:

> *The rites of the island were simplified by its elements,*
> *which changed places. The grooved sea was Achilles' garden,*
> *the ridged plot of rattling plantains carried their sense*
>
> *of the sea [...]*

With its clear, resonant language, grounding in classical heritage and emotional intensity, *Omeros* reached a wide audience, and Walcott received the Nobel Prize for Literature in 1992. He was the first Caribbean writer to be awarded this honour. The Nobel committee awarded the prize for his 'poetic oeuvre of great luminosity, sustained by a historical vision, the outcome of a multicultural commitment.' When asked about his place in the pantheon of English-language literature, Walcott said: "I am primarily, absolutely a Caribbean writer. The English language is nobody's special property. It is the property of the imagination; it is the property of the language itself. I have never felt inhibited in trying to write as well as the greatest English poets. Now that has led to a lot of provincial criticism – the Caribbean critic may say, 'You are trying to be English,' and the English critic may say, 'Welcome to the club.' These are two provincial statements at either end of the spectrum. It's not a matter of trying to be English. I am obviously a Caribbean poet."

More recently, Walcott has published *Tiepolo's Hound* (2000) – partly autobiography and partly the story of painter Camille Pissarro, and illustrated with Walcott's own paintings – and *White Egrets* (2010), a collection which won the prestigious T S Eliot Prize. Since 2009, he has also had residencies at the University of Alberta, Canada, and the University of Essex in the UK.

Poet Joseph Brodsky said of Walcott's work: 'His throbbing and relentless lines kept arriving in the English language like tidal waves, coagulating into an archipelago of poems without which the map of modern literature would effectively match wallpaper. He gives us more than himself or 'a world'; he gives us a sense of infinity embodied in the language.' One of the most important poets of the past 100 years, Derek Walcott has an almost unmatched ability to intertwine personal life events and concerns with epic forms and universal themes, along with a profound and evocative sense of place and history.

William Wordsworth (1770–1850)

'Poetry is the breath and finer spirit of all knowledge; it is the impassioned expression which is in the countenance of all Science.'

There are many who would place Wordsworth at the pinnacle of English poetic achievement. Others have been less secure about this estimation, seeing him as a poet whose early outstanding writing was not sustained into maturity. Few, however, would begrudge him the position of a very influential poet who at times wrote sublime verse.

Born in Cockermouth, Cumberland, in 1770, Wordsworth was the second of five children, one of whom, Dorothy, would become his lifelong companion and faithful scribe of his poetry. Her journals and letters provide a fascinating insight into their daily life together.

After the death of Wordsworth's mother, his father sent the children away to school. Nine-year-old William and his brothers went to the Grammar School in Hawkshead, a small town between the lakes of Coniston and Windermere. They boarded in the home of Mrs Tyson, who became a surrogate mother to the boys. William loved her very much and she gave him free rein to wander about the countryside.

Wordsworth went on to study at St John's College, Cambridge. The university did not suit the unsophisticated, unworldly young man and he lacked the motivation to study and become a man of the church or a scholar. During the generous vacations, he went on long walking tours, particularly to France and Switzerland during the great upheaval of the French Revolution. As a young student with radical ideas, he found himself with his walking friend, Robert Jones, easily able to identify with the celebrating local people and the politics of the new Republic. In time he was to change his allegiances as the reign of terror there grew more violent.

In Orleans, the youthful poet fell in love with a young woman, Annette Vallon, with whom he had a daughter. They never married, possibly because the families on both sides strongly disapproved of such a liaison, and the development of the war between England and France meant that, after his return from France, communications became impossible between them. Wordsworth wrote a long poetic reminiscence of his life experience composed in blank verse which was only published after his death in 1850 and which was posthumously entitled *The Prelude or Growth of a Poet's Mind*. While recording his hugely varied life experiences, he does not refer to the relationship with Annette and his daughter in France. This only subsequently came to light from newly discovered letters and documents in the early 20th Century.

William and his sister Dorothy settled in Nether Stowey, Somerset. Here, Wordsworth had a close friendship with Samuel Taylor Coleridge. A very intense and hugely creatively productive relationship developed between the two poets, lasting throughout their lives. They jointly published *Lyrical Ballads* in 1798. It was in this year too that Wordsworth started to write *The Prelude*. This long autobiographical poem was highly revolutionary and it is here that he expresses his almost mystical relationship with natural things. He reveals his belief that the relationship with Nature as opposed to intellectual learning is of a higher order, one which governs morality. He believed that the adult perception of the world is destructive of the mystery and innocence of the child's response to natural things and that a new language of poetry must be experienced to reflect this.

Wordsworth sought to reunite emotional responses to Nature, resisting 'the gaudiness and inane phraseology' of poetic diction and instead expressing poetic responses freshly in the ordinary language of the common person. His work shows little interest in painting verbal pictures and scenes. Rather, he seeks to communicate the emotional experience with the divine sublimity of Nature.

In 1799 Dorothy and William moved to the Lake District, where they lived in Dove Cottage in Grasmere, while Coleridge moved to nearby Keswick. It was in Grasmere that Wordsworth wrote some of his most famous poems, including *Tintern Abbey*, *Daffodils* and *Ode: Intimations of Immortality*. Wordsworth was key to the Romantic period of literature, inspiring other great poets such as Byron, Keats, Shelley and Southey. The years from 1800 to 1805 were the most creative of Wordsworth's life. In 1803 he married a lifelong friend, Mary Hutchinson, who subsequently lived with him and Dorothy and with whom he had five children. Two of these died when they were very young.

Later, the Wordsworths moved to a bigger house in the Lake District at Rydal Mount and William was appointed Distributor of Stamps. He had certain paid Inland Revenue tasks, touring the district and collecting takings to be sent to the Board of Stamps in London. He had now become very famous and was visited by many writers such as Keats and Walter Scott. In 1843, following the death of Robert Southey, he was appointed to the position of Poet Laureate, although by then his poetic inspiration was well in decline. He accepted the position as an honour only, stating that he felt unable to write for any national occasions. He died at the age of 80 at Rydal Mount, in 1850.

Wordsworth was often criticised for writing about banal subjects. At times his work may even seem like doggerel, as in the simple poem, *We Are Seven*. It is agreed that his great creative period was followed by a very swift and almost inexplicable decline in poetic power.

Perhaps readers should be aware of what Dorothy said of her brother's writing: 'When you happen to be displeased with any poem William writes, ask yourself whether you have hit upon the real tendency and true moral, and above all, never think that he writes for no reason but merely because a thing happened... ask yourself in what spirit it is written.'

In some respects Wordsworth foreshadows the later approach of psychoanalysis in his long Preface to the *Lyrical Ballads*, where he sets out to explain what poetry actually is and its effect upon the writer: 'Poetry is the spontaneous overflow of powerful feelings: it takes its origin from emotion recollected in tranquillity: the emotion is contemplated till, by a species of reaction, the tranquillity gradually disappears, and an emotion, kindred to that which was before the subject of contemplation, is gradually produced, and does itself actually exist in the mind.' In this way the act of writing evokes the original thrill and exhilaration that the poet experienced. Wordsworth was considerably ahead of his time in his artistic approach, which made him controversial in his own era.